TENACIOUS
ABUNDANCE

TENACIOUS ABUNDANCE

Simple Habits & Hacks for Being
Happy, Healthy, Wealthy & Wise

———

ANTHONY R. TRUPIANO

LIONCREST
PUBLISHING

TENACIOUS ABUNDANCE

Simple Habits & Hacks for Being Happy, Healthy, Wealthy & Wise

ISBN	978-1-5445-3232-5	*Hardcover*
	978-1-5445-3532-6	*Paperback*
	978-1-5445-3231-8	*Ebook*
	978-1-5445-3533-3	*Audiobook*

To my wife, Sally, You have made me a better person and inspired me to do great things since the day we met. Your once-in-a-lifetime love has completely changed my life in ways I could never have imagined. I will love you to eternity and back.

To our daughters, I love you and am so very proud of you both. Keep finding ways to add value to others and you will have an amazing life like your mother and I. Teach our grandkids what we taught you so they too will have an abundant life.

To my twin brother, I am so blessed to have the best brother in the entire world. Since we lost our dad, we have always remained close and had each other's backs. Thank you.

To my mother-in-law, Most people complain about their mother-in-laws; however, I feel I hit the lottery with you as my mother-in-law. Seeing how well you have lived your life, with your infectious laugh and always helping others, has been so inspiring.

To my best friends Tom and Linda Vollers, For over thirty years, you have continued to be amazing role models and supportive without hesitation. I appreciate you both so very much and your friendship means the world to me.

CONTENTS

INTRODUCTION

"There are two types of people in the world. There are people who add value and people who take away value. Always be the person that adds value and you will have a great life!"

—ROCCO TRUPIANO

Most of us want to change something about ourselves.

Maybe you're doing quite well financially, but your family relationships are in terrible shape.

Or maybe your business is going gangbusters, your family is wonderful, but your doctor says you're dangerously overweight and need medications to control your blood pressure or some other high-risk condition.

Perhaps you've fallen into a funk, unable to locate the wisdom and motivation to love life and be endlessly curious about it. Deep down you still know that life is a precious gift, but you're haunted that you might be wasting your life stressed out about things that don't ultimately matter.

I have three things to say if any of this sounds like you:

- That nagging feeling that you could be getting more out of life is 100 percent right. Life is meant for abundance in all its aspects.

- Second, *it only takes small incremental changes consistently applied to change your life dramatically.* Anyone can learn to have a life overflowing with abundance and not just financially. That might sound a little "pie-in-the-sky" to some, but it's absolutely realistic. This book is the practical, straightforward guide on how to get it.

- Last, I can say all this with total confidence because of my own lived experience. I started at the very bottom, completely broke and without direction early in my life after losing my dad as a teenager. It was sink or swim for me; I had no wealthy relatives or friends to throw me a life preserver. What I am sharing in this book are the key concepts that I used to completely turn my life around and to keep growing in abundance to this day. Tenacious habits and an abundance mindset is all you need.

HOW THIS BOOK CAME TO BE

My life has been spent in a nonstop tenacious pursuit of abundance.

For more than three decades, I have flown all across America and spent countless hours attending seminars, programs, and courses from the very top masterminds and experts in abundant living. I've invested more than $300,000 to do it and in the process have learned how to become much happier, healthier, wealthier, and wiser.

I'm also a passionate reader of books, a listener of podcasts, and a seeker of the most valuable videos and proven online information out there. I have created significant success across several industries and learned a lot along the way from both my mistakes and my triumphs in business.

In this relentless quest for abundance, I have absorbed and tested as much as possible, and in the process of all those decades I have figured out what works to create a totally abundant life. (I've also figured out what doesn't, but that's not worth writing about—I'd rather stick with telling you what actually helps!)

I decided to see if I could put what I've learned between the covers of a book. My original intention was to simply write a book for our two daughters, grandchildren, and future grandchildren as a way to guide them to live a life of tenacious abundance.

However, my wife, Sally, encouraged me to think a little bigger. "Why not share it with as many people as possible and benefit others, too?" she asked. I loved this idea and it reminded me of one of my own favorite books.

It's a classic, and I'm sure many of you have heard of it and some have no doubt read it. It's titled *Think and Grow Rich* by Napoleon Hill, and the book had a tremendous influence on me. It is still worth reading, by the way. But there are two ways it could be stronger.

One is that the language and examples are now dated, which of course is to be expected given that it was published in 1937. The second issue is that it is only focused on creating wealth (as you can tell from the title). It's fantastic advice on growing rich. But wealth is only one part of having an abundant life. You need the happiness, health, wisdom, and blessedness to go along with it.

So Sally's suggestion got me thinking in this direction. What if you had a book that served as an updated version of *Think and Grow Rich*? One that used more contemporary language and also covered how to be abundant in *all* the key areas of life?

So those are my motivations for writing this book, which all can be boiled down to giving **readers simple, actionable, and proven ways to experience a richer, more abundant life in all key areas.**

IMPORTANCE OF PROVIDING VALUE

One of the fundamental concepts that supports an abundant life is the idea of providing value to others. That's a lesson that came straight from my dad. Sadly, he died when I was sixteen, but in the relatively short time he was with me on this earth, he packed in a lifetime of lessons. Most of those lessons were by example, but he also had a few sayings that have always stuck with me.

I put one of his sayings at the beginning of this introduction because it perfectly encapsulates my burning motivation to live out my dad's advice: to be a person who adds value to the world.

I want to bring the value of tenacious abundance to the lives of others. I've seen the need for it firsthand over and over again.

Every day, I have the privilege of working with people who run their own businesses and have achieved significant financial success. They're the ones who "have it made," as the saying goes.

These are people with strong work ethics, who have created

businesses that produce something of true value. Their companies bring huge benefits to employees, customers, and society. These are good people who act with integrity and believe in giving others a fair shake.

But occasionally, they will open up to me and tell me about some aspect of their lives that bothers them. An area where abundance isn't present and where they are struggling. They want to be happier, or healthier, or wealthier, or wiser.

They also tend to be very busy people, and that can make finding solutions and implementing them extremely challenging. Of course, this applies to almost all of us, not just business owners. We have things in our lives we want to improve, but we struggle to find clear and effective solutions.

Maybe you have developed a health problem or are headed in that direction, but you can't find the time or the energy to get things turned around.

Or others struggle with their business or careers. Maybe you are successful but now you are starting to stagnate or hit a ceiling. Wisdom can also be a struggle. Even some of the smartest and savviest people I know have trouble putting life's most important things in perspective. They don't feel a sense of balance. Most of them intuitively understand things are off-kilter but don't know how to fix it and don't have the time to travel and attend seminars or workshops, read books, or listen to podcasts.

Most of us are living a life like the movie *Groundhog Day*, where we just keep repeating days over and over again and then realize later how quickly time went by. In each of these areas—happiness, health, wealth, and wisdom—many people feel lost, or at least like they're not getting nearly as much out of life as they could.

And they're right. When you neglect any of these areas, your life is less than it could be.

Without a conscious commitment to intentionally working on your happiness, health, wealth, and wisdom, you'll always default to just chasing daily problems, whether it be in your family, your business, your career, or any other key areas.

When I see anyone stuck living less than their best lives, I find it upsetting. Because it doesn't have to be that way. Not at all.

ABUNDANCE IS FOR EVERYONE

The goal is clear: to become abundant in all the key aspects of your life. Happiness. Health. Wealth. Wisdom. And then put it all together and live a blessed life. But just because the goal is clear, that does not mean we know the path to it.

What stops us from finding the path?

I think many people have the idea that abundance has a lot to do with luck, genetics, or environment. And sometimes people just envision being abundant in one area but think they will forever be deficient in others.

Unfortunately, some have even convinced themselves that this can never change. They assume it is the best they can do. *"Hey, a few areas of my life are going fairly well, and the rest…well, what are you going to do?"*

This book is about real, practical things you can do to invite the overflowing gift of abundance into your life. It is for everyone because anyone who wants more in their life can receive it. I'm here to tell you that abundance really is possible in all key areas of your life. And even though you can't create it instantly in every area all at once, you can begin to turn things around right away by implementing a few simple habits, hacks, or beliefs in each area.

You do not have to be 100 percent convinced right now that you can have abundance throughout your entire life. All you have to do is be willing to be open minded enough to read and take action and allow the actual results to change your mind.

Of course, as the title of this book implies, I don't just want you to be abundant. I want you to have tenacious abundance. What do I mean when I say that?

One part of being tenacious is the **idea of extreme persistence**. It is a theme you will find throughout the book. The habits and hacks I recommend need to be done consistently for at least a few months before you can call them your own (which doesn't mean you won't start feeling benefits right away—you will). **Realistically, habits take a minimum of ninety days (and often more) to get wired into your system, much longer than the twenty-one to thirty days that the self-help industry touts as long enough to establish a new habit.**

Tenacity is also an attitude, a mindset of moving firmly toward your goal of happiness, health, wealth, and wisdom. You commit to a cohesive effort, with your life choices all pointed toward making you a person of abundance.

I also want you to believe tenaciously that you deserve abundance and can get it. Do not let anyone or anything shake you from that belief. If you can master that belief, you will be unstoppable.

HOW TO GET THE MOST OUT OF THIS BOOK

This book is purposely designed for easy reading. I wrote it for busy people who do not have time for a lot of fluff or padding. I read *a lot* of books on living a better life, and even many of the ones I love tend to go on way longer than necessary. Instead of sticking with a core of actionable strategies and telling a few interesting and enlightening stories, too many pages are devoted to endlessly discussing the research or repeating things past the point of usefulness. I find myself having to skim through and do the work of pulling out what is important.

I will make a few key points more than once for emphasis, but this whole book is dedicated to giving you the strategies and tactics that are the "best of the best" and cutting out anything that is not necessary. Along the way, I will tell you some stories that I hope will illuminate and reinforce what I'm saying (and maybe entertain you a bit, too!). The content is designed to give you maximum value from every minute you spend on it.

This book also does not have to be read all the way through from beginning to end to get tremendous benefit from it. It is structured so you can start with any chapter and get something out of it immediately. For example, if health is a problem area for you, read Chapter 2 ("I Am Healthy") and find at least one thing you can implement right away.

You can go even shorter if you want. Skim a chapter and find a section that speaks to you about something you want to change. **There are a lot of subheadings in each chapter, so you can easily find bite-sized advice that you can digest and then take action on.** Everything is created to be user-friendly to the busy reader, even if you are not reading the book straight through. If you are truly pressed for time, the most succinct summaries of the key ideas can be found in the **"Power of 3s"** at the end of most chapters.

That said, reading it from page one all the way to the end will unlock even more benefits. My hope is that you might do that and that then this book earns a permanent place on your nightstand or desk. That you use it like a user manual for the abundant life, opening it up and reading any section that applies to your life in that moment and getting what you need to get and stay on track.

COMMON SENSE IS NOT COMMONLY PRACTICED

As you will discover, most of the timeless wisdom, habits, hacks, and beliefs are common sense sounding.

Some reject perfectly sound advice because they say it is "too simple." Or that it's "just common sense." But that is to miss the key point: you have to actually practice it to get the results. **Never confuse common sense with common practice!**

What I have done in this book is taken the best wisdom, strategies, and tactics I know for a tenaciously abundant life and distilled it down into something even the busiest person has time to both grasp and implement. Much of it is common sense, but so few use what they know to take action.

You have probably heard the advice that we all have exactly the same twenty-four hours in a day and that life is short and we need to make the most of it. Most people nod and agree but then fail to let the truth of those statements sink in.

The most abundant people I have met and studied never underestimate the importance of using their time wisely. That's why the crux of this book is to help you develop habits, hacks, and beliefs that can be done by anyone and can fit into any schedule. Most people seem to think that the truly successful and abundant have some sort of secret sauce or magic formula that catapults them to the moon. **However, in reality it is five to ten key habits that you can adopt to create amazing abundance in your life.**

This book is to help you discover and implement your key habits and hacks for tenacious abundance in all areas of your life, using the same twenty-four hours that everyone has.

Since 1991, I have been on a quest to live a life that hits on all cylinders of fulfillment for myself and my family. Everything I will mention in this book I have road tested, and now I recommend it to you because…it works! One thing you will not find in this book is fluff, exaggerations, or advice that wastes your time.

MY TOP 3% SECRET

You may notice throughout the book that I use the number 3 a lot. It's my favorite number, as in the saying "It's as simple as 1, 2, 3," and I always love simple and powerful. You'll see this number in the Power of 3s that sum up chapters and in the 3 Anchor Method to create your perfect day (see Chapter 5).

The number 3 can also serve as a foundation for thinking about excellence. In the year 2000, I gave myself the goal of being in the top 3 percent of everything I do. It was a way to challenge myself to improve in all areas.

Some would say go for the top 1 percent, but to do that in every area might become an endless chase. You could also aim for the top 10 percent, and there would be nothing wrong with that worthy goal. But I have found the idea of aiming for the top 3 percent to be the right fit, challenging enough to keep you inspired but not so over the top as to be too frustrating.

In some areas, exactly what would be the top 3 percent might be hard to define precisely (like wisdom, for example). My hope is that as you read this book, you will get a good feel for what it means to be in the top 3 percent in any area and how to get there. Thinking of being in the top 3 percent has been a good guiding light that has served me very well, and I hope you will take the same spirit toward abundance as you make your way through this book.

I should also note that I never say my goal is to be better than 97 percent of people. To phrase it that way would be to miss the point. It would make it about beating others and trying to be above them. **My top 3% goal is always about living up to my high standards and improving myself, not about being better or above others.**

· · ·

It's time to start on this journey. I want you to find the same tenacious abundance I have discovered through listening and learning from others and from living and experiencing the abundant life myself for over three decades. Let's start with how to bring more happiness into your life.

CHAPTER 1

I AM HAPPY

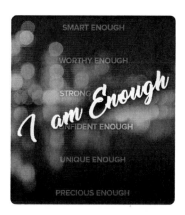

Why aren't I happier?

This question haunts many people. It is something that trips up even some of the most successful people you will ever meet. If this is something you wonder yourself, do not feel alone. **You are not.**

But do not just accept it either, because there are ways to be happier starting right now. This is your opportunity to finally do something about it. I promise you, if you read this chapter and take it to heart and take action, *you will get happier.*

But where should you start?

This chapter is loaded with practical solutions, but first I want to give you three principles for being happy. Before we get to specific tactics and hacks, it is crucial to grasp these fundamentals of happiness:

- **Happiness is an inside job.** You cannot control outward circumstances or other people's behavior.

- **You need to unconditionally love yourself.** That might sound a little corny to some at first, but keep reading to understand how important this is.

- **You need to realize** *you are enough.* The nagging sense of never being good enough causes so much misery in this world. Learn to overcome it, and your happiness will skyrocket.

Let's look at each of these principles in a little more depth.

You first need to accept the limits of your control. For example, many people let the news of the day get them all riled up, despite not being able to do anything about 99.9 percent of it. (I know, because I let it happen to me until I cut it out of my life.)

Or maybe you have someone in the family who every time you visit, they are a machine of negativity and conflict. We allow ourselves to get twisted in knots over their behavior, even though nothing we do or say will stop them from being negative.

Later in this chapter, we will talk more specifically about how to address this, but for now, just reflect on how many times you allow what is out of your control to make you miserable.

Once you have this insight, you can see the next logical conclusion: true and lasting happiness is always an inside job. Unfortunately, the default position for most of us is, "*If only I had* [fill in the blank: more money, that job, a connection, etc.],

I would be happy." This mindset will forever put happiness outside your own control and leave it to luck and circumstances. And even when things "go your way," you will find that kind of happiness is typically fleeting. Think about it. How many times have you felt happy, only to find it quickly dissipates and then you claim you need some other outer condition to be met before you can be happy again?

Since happiness comes from inside, that means you start at your inner core. And that means loving yourself unconditionally. At first, that might sound too vague and intangible to be useful, but I can tell you from experience that there are very practical ways to love yourself. One of the best habits for this are affirmations.

YOU ARE ENOUGH

I have done affirmations for most of my adult life, and they are an amazing tool for creating more peace and happiness in your life.

So when I was listening to an episode of the Ed Mylett podcast and his guest Howard Behar mentioned he had an affirmation he'd been repeating to himself for fifty years, I dialed my attention in and became really curious. Here was a man who had been president of Starbucks for twenty-one years and had attained gigantic success. He was sharing an affirmation he said *every day for fifty years*. Seemed like a good idea to listen to what he had to say.

After sharing his affirmation, he did something else extraordinary. He shared his personal phone number and email. The host was flabbergasted and asked if he wasn't concerned about being flooded with all kinds of requests and questions.

Behar explained that he gave out this information all the time, and he found very few people ever reached out. It always astounds me how many people do not take advantage of these kinds of opportunities. (By the way, in this same tradition and spirit, I have included my email and phone number at the back of this book.) I recommend reading his book *It's Not About the Coffee* and visiting howardbehar.com.

I love to reach out to mega-successful people and learn as much as I can from them. So, of course, I sent him an email with a few questions and he graciously replied right away.

One of the things I asked him was how much of his success he attributed to repeating this same affirmation for fifty years. He said what he thought it brought to his life was a peace of mind, and that had been one of the pillars of his success. Here was a man who had taken Starbucks from a handful of stores and built it into one of the most recognized businesses in the world. There must have been a lot of great challenges and stress along the way. But this affirmation kept him at peace.

I immediately implemented this affirmation in my own life. I already had a high level of happiness at that point, but I have discovered this affirmation is special. It is permission to feel at peace with the abundance already in your life and lays the foundation for even more peace and happiness to enter your life.

Here is the affirmation:

I am enough. I have enough. I do enough.

My recommendation is to implement this affirmation in your life starting today. Say this affirmation once in the morning and once in the evening while looking in the mirror. Also, use it at any time during the day when you are feeling stressed, overwhelmed, or being overly critical of yourself.

This affirmation reminds me of a scene in the movie *Planes, Trains, and Automobiles*. If you haven't seen it, do yourself a favor and find it and watch it. My wife and I both consider it one of our favorite movies. (She always cries during the last scene when they play the song "Everytime You Go Away." Not me, although sometimes I do get something in my eye.)

There's a particular scene where Steve Martin's character is being especially mean, and he unloads all his frustration by criticizing the John Candy character (named Dell). Dell responds:

"Well, you think what you want about me...I like me. My wife likes me. My customers like me. 'Cause I'm the real article. What you see is what you get."

What a beautiful example of knowing you are enough. Dell, for all his problems, understands something about happiness that many miss.

It is hard for me to overemphasize how much affirmations have done for my happiness in life, and how effective this one is in particular. Please do yourself the favor of implementing it and sticking with it every day. It is so valuable that I'm going to repeat it one more time in hopes that you will begin applying it right now. Say it out loud and see if you do not sense its power:

I am enough. I have enough. I do enough.

I have no doubt that at least some of you are skeptical at the moment. Could something as simple as saying this affirmation, every day, multiple times a day, be so crucial to your happiness and your mindset? The answer is yes. Howard Behar has proven it with his peace of mind while building amazing success. I can personally attest to its power in my own life.

If you have some initial reservations, that's fine. You can still commit to saying it every day into the mirror, multiple times a day. Make the effort to do it regularly and sincerely and see if it does not overcome your doubts.

Although I want you to make this your number one affirmation, do not stop there.

POWER OF AFFIRMATIONS

There are more affirmations that I use regularly to keep myself feeling abundant and happy. My hope is that you will use these examples and/or create affirmations that best suit your own life and circumstances.

One I have used for many years is **"I love my life. I love my wife. I have no strife."** Rhyme can be a powerful aid in remembering and reinforcing affirmations. If you are going to create customized affirmations, use rhyme when possible.

Affirmations should also be about things that are fundamental to your happiness. This one reminds me of how important my marriage is to me and has helped me stay married and happy with the woman of my dreams for three decades and counting.

I also write every day in my gratitude journal and on mirrors that **"I am enough,"** that **"I am abundant,"** and that **"I am blessed."** I also recite this many times during my day.

Notice also that I use "I am" in front of most of my affirmations. This is very important because that way, it doesn't sound like you are just wishing and hoping. Instead, you are saying it as if you already possess the quality you are affirming.

I also do a simple affirmation often during the day that is simply, **"All is well."** Our brains have a tendency to search for things to worry about, and this dynamic needs to be offset. When you feel stress creeping in, answer it with, "All is well."

Of course, there may be times when all is not well. I still encourage you to say it. You are not doing it to lie to yourself or ignore a problem that may need solving. It's simply a good reminder that even in the midst of challenges, you can remain on an even keel, at peace knowing you will find your way to a solution.

It is good to create affirmations about the most important roles in our lives. For example, you should look in the mirror every morning and say, "I'm a great husband. I'm a great father. I'm a great brother. I'm a great person." (Obviously, you will want to customize it to your own relationships.) This affirmation is great because it positively acknowledges what you are already doing right but also serves as a reminder throughout the rest of your day to live up to what you are expressing.

I sometimes get asked, "But what if I haven't been a good _____?" Then you adjust to the situation. Let's say you have not been a good brother or sister. First, forgive yourself. Next, send a note or make a phone call and apologize to your sibling and say you want to repair the relationship. Now your affirmation can be, "I am going to be a better brother/sister." Your affirmations can be positive while still being real.

Here are a few tips to keep affirmations front and center in your life:

- Write them on a mirror using mirror markers.

- Set your cell phone background to be an affirmation and/or set your phone to give you alerts that contain the affirmation.

- Set it as your screensaver and/or background for your computer.

- Put key affirmations on your vision board (there is an explanation of vision boards in Chapter 4).

THE PERSON IN THE MIRROR SHOULD BE YOUR BEST FRIEND

It is not just what we say out loud that counts. We should also give ourselves visually affirming cues, which are very powerful for our brains. It helps us internalize a positive mindset that reminds us to love ourselves unconditionally.

Here are a few you can do:

- Do a superhero pose in front of the mirror at least once daily (bonus points if you play the theme from *Superman* while you do it). The benefits of this have been proven scientifically by Harvard researchers Dana Carney, Amy Cuddy, and Andy Yap in their study "Power Posing: Brief Nonverbal Displays Affect Neuroendocrine Levels and Risk Tolerance" published in *Psychological Science* in 2010.

- When you do affirmations in front of a mirror (which you should do a minimum of once daily), always end by giving yourself two thumbs-up. This is like reinforcing the affirmation with an exclamation point. Remember, this can be done with any mirror you use throughout the day, including your rearview mirror, work bathroom mirror, and even a public restroom mirror.

- Smile in the mirror. Every time you look in any mirror, give yourself a smile, the same as you would when you greet a friend. Tell yourself you are doing great!

STOP BULLYING YOURSELF

I find that most of us are natural bullies. Not of others (although of course those people exist, too—avoid them). What I am talking about is bullying ourselves.

How many times do we say to ourselves after making a mistake, "You stupid idiot" and then go on to berate ourselves at some length for our misstep?

How often do we keep turning our past actions over and over in our minds, sometimes for things that happened years or even decades ago—things we would have long ago forgiven a friend for?

The truth is that most of us say negative things all the time to ourselves that we would never say to anyone else. For some reason, we accept bullying self-talk as normal. This quietly eats away at our confidence and does damage to our happiness.

You can stop bullying yourself by following this rule for self-talk: if you would not say it to your best friend or loved ones, do not say it to yourself.

This is one of the best ways to train your mind and heart to love yourself unconditionally. If a friend made a major misstep, would you berate him and hurl abuse his way, or would you look for ways to build him back up and truly help? If he came to you for advice for making a change in his life, would you tell him all the reasons he was stupid and why his plans won't work?

Do you follow your friends around constantly, being hyper critical about even their smallest thoughts and actions? Of course not. But isn't that exactly what we often do to ourselves?

Here's what you should do to begin breaking yourself of these mental habits. Pick a day this week and notice every time you engage in negative self-talk in your head. You may be surprised by how often it happens. But then I want you to go one step further. For each instance of negative self-talk, imagine what you would say to a family member or friend whom you love unconditionally. Replace your negative talk with that. Then rinse and repeat.

Keep working on this daily until it becomes ingrained. Stop bullying yourself!

START YOUR DAY WITH ONE SINCERE COMPLIMENT

Here is a great thing to do every morning. Reach out to a client, friend, family member, or even a complete stranger and pay them a sincere compliment. Do not be motivated by business if it is a client; do not try to sell them anything when you reach out. **Whoever you choose, make it about truly connecting with another human being with a genuine compliment.**

I have trained myself to do this on a regular basis and the benefits are gigantic, both for the happiness of my day and spreading an abundance mindset to others. The impact you make is huge; no one expects to be given thoughtful compliments out of the blue.

You will find yourself reminded of how grateful you are for the people in your life, and the recipient will get more joy in their own life.

Here is another great way to connect with others that you can use as an alternative to the compliment: reach out to somebody and ask about their family, or if they have gone through a tough time recently, ask them how they are holding up. Create the intention to show sincere caring for someone else, and then express it to them. There's no need to get fancy with this; just call them up and have a natural conversation about how things are going. **Since the number one human need is to be heard, it is enough to just be a good listener and let them tell you what's on their mind.**

Do either or both of these at least once a day and you'll see your connections grow stronger, which provides one of the biggest boosts to happiness imaginable.

Now let's turn to getting more happiness in your life using addition by subtraction. It is time to cut out the things that do not add to your happiness.

TURN OFF THE NEWS

I completely stopped watching the news and it changed my life. Both my wife and daughters commented soon after I stopped watching that I seemed less tense, and that was absolutely how I felt.

Think about the business model for news. They make the majority of their money through advertising. **Their formula is,**

more eyeballs = more money. And how do you get more viewers and clicks? Negativity, conflict, and anger are the easiest way to draw us in, and so that is exactly what they deliver.

This calls back to the idea early in this chapter. You cannot expect to be consistently happy as long as you allow outside forces that you do not control to impact your emotional state.

Despite knowing this, I still allowed myself to fall into the trap of letting the political news get me fired up too often. Then one day, I got very upset about a particular story, and it suddenly hit me that I had no control over the news and I immediately cut it out of my life and have not looked back. The media industry serves its advertisers, like the pharmaceutical and financial industries and whoever else pays them. It certainly is not there to serve our interests or well-being.

If you would like to add some balance to the stories you read, I recommend a great website, www.goodnewsnetwork.org, that focuses on positive and inspirational stories.

LIMITING SOCIAL MEDIA

Similar to the television news, social media can drown us in negativity. Even when it is not negative, it will seriously eat into time that could be better spent on activities that make us happier, healthier, and more productive.

My solution has been to cut out all social media except LinkedIn, which I use for business purposes. You might not want to go that far, but at a minimum, put yourself on a strict time budget for time spent on social media.

Whether you decide to eliminate social media or just severely limit it, do it for a full month, and then ask yourself if you feel better and happier for having done it. If the answer is yes—and it almost always is—then stick with it!

Control your surfing of websites, too. My tactic is to limit myself to a very few trusted sources of information and keep the time I spend on those websites to a minimum.

As a bonus, the more you control your time on social media and the internet, the better you protect your privacy as well. Social media is filled with people announcing all kinds of things about themselves, including when they are on vacation and the house is empty. The internet is loaded with sites tracking everything they can about you. So be intentional as to what you need to search and cut out everything else.

CUT OUT PEOPLE WHO ARE BAD ENERGY

Too many people are afraid to cut ties with people who make them miserable, and for reasons they never examine.

For example, I think some people who run their own businesses are afraid to fire clients and customers because...well, they are paying money and it is something "you just don't do." I disagree. I have fired clients, even some who were quite profitable. These were clients whom we did our best to serve, which they returned with a steady stream of negativity and bad energy.

Of course, I am not suggesting this as something that you would do on a regular basis or that everyone you serve has to constantly show you love and appreciation. Situations like this can have a lot of different nuances. My point is simply that we do not have to hold it as sacred that we never fire a client or customer. If they never show any appreciation for the value you bring, you may be doing them a favor, too.

You can then focus on bringing even more value to those who love what you do for them, and on adding more customers who appreciate what you do.

Much of the above applies to family, too. This is another area where some people get stuck thinking that cutting someone out of their life is impossible. Of course, family relationships and obligations are tricky, and except in the most extreme circumstances, you may not feel comfortable cutting off all contact. We all know the saying that you can choose your friends but not your family.

But whatever the individual circumstance, it is always possible to limit your exposure to family members who bring bad energy. **Set boundaries for yourself and for them and stick to them.** You will thank me for this advice if you have the courage to set limits with negative family members.

Friends are similar. You may find yourself in relationships where you have evolved in different directions. If every time you are with a particular person you feel dragged down or they encourage unhealthy choices, that is a danger sign. **The commonly expressed idea that you are the average of the five people you spend the most time with is true, so consider who you are hanging around.**

I hope it goes without saying that all of the above applies only to those who have made self-pity, bad energy, and complaining a regular habit. I am not talking about anyone who is simply going through a tough time and needs your support and understanding.

To summarize all this succinctly: With family, friends, and business relationships, *be intentional* about whom you spend time with and be aware of their influence on you. Increase those who bring more positive energy into your life, and decrease or cut out those who are pulling you down.

RELATIONSHIP LIFE PRESERVERS

So much of our happiness comes down to the health of our relationships, and that is particularly true if you are married or in a serious relationship. I find that people who always want to believe the grass is greener on the other side of the fence do not invest time caring for their own side and then wonder why it becomes a wasteland. **In other words, stop focusing on someone else's lawn and make sure you are watering, fertilizing, and tending to your own lawn.**

You need to pay attention and be active in caring for the health of your relationship with your spouse. Here's a list of dos and don'ts that my wife and I have used to keep our marriage abundantly happy.

DO'S:

- Do small daily things, like spelling out messages in Q-tips and planting hidden love notes, or occasional surprises "just because."

- Do everyday things together whenever possible (the grocery store, the mall, errands, etc.).

- Do have a date night at least once a week.

- Do collaborate on your parenting. Both parents should both be rowing the boat in the same direction.

It's a common error these days to try to be your kid's friend. Be their parents and let them find their friends at school and among peers (like we did!).

- Do respect each other and back up your spouse on decisions.

- It might sound a bit cliché, but flowers and candy surprises never get old!

- Every year, ask your spouse if they are happy with the marriage and how your life together is going. Are there any things they would like to change or work on?

- Share in household chores. Do not think of anything as exclusively a woman's or man's job. Instead, the attitude should always be to help out each other as much as possible.

- Spouses come first, then friends second, not the other way around.

DON'TS:

- Don't go to bed upset or angry with each other. Talk it out and settle before going to sleep.

- Don't evade responsibility if you mess up. Apologize quickly and sincerely and move forward.

- Don't expect perfection from your spouse. Instead, make each other laugh every day, and make light of mistakes.

- Don't make issues bigger than they really are, and always focus on solutions.

- Don't speak poorly about your spouse or significant other with anyone, NEVER EVER!

BE RESOURCEFUL IN ALL AREAS OF YOUR LIFE

I am convinced through observation and by my own life that the happiest people in the world are those who understand they need to add value to others and are resourceful about it.

This is where being tenacious comes in.

You might say, "But Anthony, I am tenacious and resourceful. Whenever my business (or career) faces a challenge, I put in whatever time and thought is necessary to surmount it." That's terrific; it really is.

But what I often find—and this applies to all of us at one time or another—is we forget to be that resourceful in other areas of our life.

That problem you are having with your brother, are you putting in as much tenacity and resourcefulness for healing that relationship as you do when figuring out a cash flow problem? Are you being as tenacious in lowering your high blood sugar as you are with finding new customers?

If more of us trusted ourselves to be tenaciously resourceful about every key part of our life, the quantity of happiness in the world would go way up. In my experience, we are all a lot better at coming up with great solutions than we give ourselves credit for. We also want to solve the problems of others with the best of intentions, but sometimes the bigger favor is to say, "I trust you to solve this because I know you can do it."

My recommendation: write down the top problem in your life right now, no matter what it is. Money, health, relationship—anything holding you back from abundance. Now spend thirty minutes writing down solutions. Drill down to ideas that are practical and then pick out a specific plan of action. You might be surprised by how resourceful you are when you take the time and trust yourself. **When you are forced to come up with solutions and a plan of action, it pushes you to start asking better questions or to find someone who can help you.** All of this will generate some great ideas.

HAPPINESS IS AN INSIDE JOB

Some of you are going to struggle at first in trying to make changes that make you happier. That's okay. Here are a few simple things you can do if you have trouble believing you can really make changes.

The first thing I want you to do, and pardon my French, **is question sh*tty beliefs**. Example: Let's say you were previously married and it ended in divorce. You remarried and now this second marriage is hitting a rough patch. You feel the same old dynamics kicking in.

Here's the miserable belief you formulate: I'm not a good husband. I'm just not the kind of person who can have a happy married relationship.

That's a sh*tty belief, and you need to question it. Ask yourself, are you really a bad husband? Or is it really that you need to make a few behavioral changes? **Changing your beliefs from harsh self-criticism to a productive search for solutions can make all the difference.** For example, ask things like, "What actions add up to create a good husband-wife relationship?" At one point, you loved this person enough to marry them; what are you both doing differently in your relationship now that is causing so much friction?

Miserable beliefs have a common quality. Whenever you find yourself saying, "I'm just not good at _____" or you in some way insult yourself like, "I'm just an idiot when it comes to making money decisions," you've got it wrong. Negative catch-all statements make it too easy to begin spiraling down into a victim mindset.

Anytime you find yourself making broad negative comments about yourself, question that belief immediately. Ask if the belief is really true, or am I just not putting the effort in to replace it with a more empowering belief?

The key is to avoid self-pity, name-calling, and other emotion-based reactions to negative circumstances. Focus on practical solutions and lessons learned and then move on. That's common sense, but unfortunately it's not common practice.

The other big obstacle to sustained happiness is thinking that it should happen faster. There is a piece of folk "wisdom" that circulates endlessly on the internet and in some self-help books that a habit takes twenty-one days to become fixed in your life. I'm sorry, but that is just BS.

You have been doing something your whole life and in twenty-one days you are going to completely imprint a new habit? No way. It takes months at a minimum, and sometimes you need to do something for a full year for it to become totally ingrained.

(If you struggle maintaining daily habits, I recommend reading Chapter 5.)

Remember most of all that being happy is an inside job, a choice to take daily actions to make yourself happier. Too many people walk around trying to be different people in different situations. Life is much simpler—and happier—when you are the same person across the board.

This hit home to me when I once heard Oprah interviewing Kenny Rogers about his friendship with Dolly Parton. Oprah wondered what made her special to him.

I have never forgotten Rogers's answer. He said the person Dolly thinks she is, the person most people believe she is, and the actual person that Dolly is day to day are all the same person. This is important to keep in mind whenever you interact and communicate with others: always be the genuine YOU. In other words: **The person you think you are, the person others think you are, and who you really are should all be the same person.**

THE POWER OF 3s
CHAPTER SUMMARY

Top Ways to Implement the Concepts in This Chapter

Three Key Habits/Hacks

1. Use a superhero pose in the mirror every morning and tell yourself any/or all of the following: "I am enough, have enough, and do enough." "I love my life and have no strife." "I am a great husband/wife, I am a great father/mother, I am a great son/daughter, I am a great brother/sister, I am a great friend, I am great at [whatever your occupation is]," and then finish with "I am a great person and I unconditionally love myself."

2. Start your day with a sincere compliment or a way to help someone else have a great day. Helping others helps you.

3. Surround yourself with people who give you energy and add value in your life and it is very important that you are reciprocating.

Three Key Beliefs

1. I am enough, have enough, and do enough.

2. I love my life and have no strife.

3. The person in the mirror is my lifelong best friend.

Three Key Questions

1. Whom do I love, who loves me?

2. What in my life is going great right now?

3. Who could I sincerely compliment today via a text, email, or phone call?

CHAPTER 2

I AM HEALTHY

I am going to tell you about the worst day of my life.

As you can already probably tell, I am a very positive, happy person, so it might seem odd to start a chapter by sharing this. But it is an important story. It will tell you a little more about who I am and what my motivations are. **Most of all, I hope it encourages you to take care of your own health.**

The last morning I saw my dad, he was sitting in front of our wood stove because he felt so cold. It was in the middle of a cold New Jersey winter, but something wasn't right. His ankles were swollen, and he had been feeling run-down lately. I had just turned sixteen at the time and did not know enough to understand that these were all symptoms of a serious heart issue. His heart wasn't strong enough to pump the blood back up from his ankles.

My dad did not know that either, or at least not how severe his problem was. He was a former Golden Gloves boxer, and we all viewed him as a vital and powerful guy. He had been looking a little frail lately, but surely this durable guy would be fine.

It was not until a few years later as I entered adulthood that I put together the full story of why our family health history should have made us more concerned.

THE TOUGHEST DAY OF MY LIFE

It was a cold January day in 1982. The morning started off with me being nervous because of a big high school wrestling match that day. I had been on the team for two months and found I had a talent for it. I was thrilled that in my first season as a wrestler, I had beat out a senior for a spot on varsity in my weight class. But wrestling varsity meant I would be taking on the best opponents. And today, the kid I was wrestling had a reputation as one of the best in the state, so I was feeling a little unsure of myself.

My dad, sitting in front of that wood stove, gifted me some of his trademark common sense that morning. He asked, "The other kid will weigh the same as you, right?" I told him yes. It was his way of reminding me not to beat myself before the match even started by building my opponent up into more than he was.

Then he added the kicker: "And you've got more heart than him." Wow. Talk about creating a mindset shift with a few simple words.

That was vintage Rocco Trupiano. He had a seventh-grade education but more common sense than any other man I have known. My dad had to leave school to start working when his own dad fell ill while he was in middle school. Without much education and with no money or connections, he still eventually owned three gas stations. My twin brother and I grew up in the family business, learning a healthy work ethic early. We were pumping gas at his stations by age six.

As he began not feeling well, my dad decided to sell the stations and went to work for someone else. Although we weren't rich, we had my dad's paycheck and his steady hand to guide us.

I sure appreciated that guidance that morning, and off I went to school and later my wrestling match.

* * *

When the bus pulled in after returning from the away match, I was the only kid who did not have a parent waiting to pick me up. I was especially disappointed that no one was there because I couldn't wait to tell my dad that his advice had worked. I not only won my match; I shut the guy out.

With no ride, I did what everyone else did back before cell phones and texting. I found a pay phone and dialed zero for the operator to make a collect call home.

The way it worked was whoever answered the phone would refuse to accept the charges but would be signaled that I was ready to be picked up. But that night, the phone just rang and rang. I stood in the cold for three hours until finally a neighbor showed up near midnight.

On the ride home, the neighbor broke the news that my father had suffered a heart attack. I got home just as my brother and mom were arriving back from the hospital. My dad was not doing well, they said. My mom returned to the hospital.

At 3:00 a.m., she returned home again. My dad had died of heart failure at age forty-five.

To say we were completely devastated would be an understatement. Besides losing my amazing father whom I considered my best friend, we discovered Dad had not paid the premium on his life insurance and had no retirement plan. And my mother had never worked a day in her life.

Life became very different, very fast.

I would arrive home from wrestling practice and help my brother chop wood to keep the wood stoves going for heat. I also had to get a job as a janitor's assistant to help with food costs at home. We went to local truck stops to fill our own cans with diesel to dump into our oil tank that provided us with hot water because we could not afford an oil delivery.

Many people began to shun us, as if my dad's death was something that made us lesser people. A particularly devastating instance was when the friend whom I spent the most time with was told by his mother to stay away from me because I was fatherless and probably would not amount to much.

Thankfully, not everyone abandoned us. At the end of the wrestling season, I had a burning desire to become the best wrestler I could. I asked my coach what the best wrestling camp in the country was, and he answered without hesitation that it was the Iowa Intensive Wrestling camp.

I immediately went to our neighbors, a family of dairy farmers, and asked for $320 to attend this camp that would be held at Lock Haven University. I promised that I would come back after camp and work the rest of the summer to pay off my debt. These neighbors, the Cliffords, were just amazing people who were unhesitatingly generous in agreeing to help. I consider that camp the start of my journey to a lifelong commitment to tenacious abundance.

*   *   *

When I reflect on this story, I see how this time of suffering shaped me in two important ways. For one, it gave my entrepreneurial spirit an eventual direction. At a young age, I had already decided that I would be the head of Trupiano Corporation someday. I just did not know what that corporation would do. I fulfilled my promise to have my own business, and what I do is help people with investments, retirement, and insurance. **I never want anyone to be left in dire financial straits when someone passes like what happened to my family.**

It also shaped my passion for being abundantly healthy. I said earlier that it took me several years to get a larger perspective on my family health history. Being in insurance, you come to understand that family history is one of the biggest risk factors for health and mortality. My grandfather had died at an early age. The story was, he had collapsed walking down a street in Brooklyn, I think around the age of sixty. It seemed so unlikely because he always reminded me of the famous fitness guru of the time, Jack Lalanne. Just so strong and healthy-looking on the outside.

I also had an uncle who passed away from a heart attack at age thirty-six. This connection with genetics wasn't as well understood or communicated back when my dad was struggling with his own health.

Today, we do know those connections, and ever since, I have worked hard to take thorough care of my health to avoid a similar fate. Since nothing can bring back my dad, I would at least be pleased if his story inspires even one person reading this to get healthier and live longer. One of my biggest motivations in telling you this story is to help you avoid your family having to suffer through the agony of being robbed of years or even decades without you around. In the United States, medical expenses cause nearly 67 percent of personal bankruptcies, so it pays to stay healthy. The concepts, resources, and exercises that make up the rest of this chapter are a simple way to get started on a healthier trajectory.

So let's start talking about how to get healthier by busting a big myth that keeps too many busy people from taking better care of themselves.

BUSTING A HARMFUL MYTH

I meet successful people all the time who buy into a huge myth that will shave years off their life and is harming the quality of their life right now.

Myth: I have to choose between running my business/ building a great career OR focusing on my health. I don't have enough time for both.

I completely understand how hard people work to build a business or to grow their career. You will get no argument from me about the time and dedication necessary. But this does NOT mean you have to sacrifice your health to do it.

I get why some people believe you have to choose one or the other. Maybe you had a long day in the office and you are tired and hungry and want to get home as soon as possible. That McDonald's you pass on the way home seems like a pretty attractive choice under these circumstances. Try not to think that already today you had a lunch of pizza chased by a Pepsi and ate it in a rush. Two fast, unhealthy meals in a row, and it happens more than you care to admit.

Exercise is also a problem. Finding time to go to the gym regularly when your days are packed? Forget about it.

Remember what is at stake, though. **If you are not around to enjoy all that money you piled up for retirement, what's the point?** When you reach the time to enjoy your family and the fruits of your labor and you have lost your mobility or other capacities, what then?

There is no reason to choose. Superhuman effort will not be needed. I am going to give you some simple changes to make in your lifestyle that can be accomplished by anyone who wants to put in a reasonable effort. Not only that, if you make these changes, you will have *more* energy for work, not less.

Before I give you more specifics, we first need to get rid of the number one mindset obstacle to getting healthier.

RID YOURSELF OF THE "ALL OR NOTHING" MENTALITY

Here is something that afflicts so many people who want to make the transition to a healthier lifestyle: they want to make a bunch of radical changes all at once.

This is the classic New Year's resolution fallacy, where January 1 or some other arbitrary date is supposedly the day to completely flip the switch. Diet will go from mostly junk to totally healthy foods, calories will immediately be strictly limited, and a promise will be made to go to the gym for an hour workout every other day.

You may not go quite that far, but does that sound a little familiar? If it does, do not beat yourself up; it is a common mistake. Trying to make too many massive changes all at once is doomed to failure. It traps you in a mindset where the inevitable first slip up will send you right back to your old habits.

Habits expert James Clear likes to make the point that **you need to fall in love with the process instead of the outcome,** which I think very much applies here. He uses the example of having books on your nightstand and reading regularly. He says the goal is not to finish reading a particular book; the goal is to become a reader. In a similar way, the goal is not to accomplish a hard-core crazy workout or eat healthy for a day; **it's to become a person who makes healthy choices consistently and a person who enjoys fitness.**

For the rest of the chapter, you will find lots of tips, hacks, and strategies for making small but impactful changes that you can make one at a time, until they grow into healthy habits that create massive change in how you feel. Pick the one that most resonates with you and take action.

REMIND YOURSELF OF THE REASONS YOU WANT TO BE HEALTHY

Being abundantly healthy means you have to be tenacious about it. An initial burst of motivation will not deliver enough fuel to keep you on track long term.

The best way to maintain that tenacity is to get explicit about why you want to be healthy. I cannot hand you a set of reasons that motivate you specifically; it always has an element of the personal. But reflecting on the following points will help you create your own health mission statement.

- Why are you working so hard? Is one of the reasons to enjoy your later years with family, friends, and enjoying an active lifestyle? Is the way you are treating your body right now setting you up to be physically able to do what you envision in retirement?

- What would it be like for your family and friends to experience your death sooner than if you had taken better care of yourself?

- How can you turn what you just reflected on into a positive mission statement?

- What could you start doing now that would extend your life another ten years?

Now let's get even more practical. **Health is really an equation based on two things: what you put in your body and how often/how well you move that body**. We'll begin with what you are putting in your body.

FEELING FIT IS BETTER THAN EATING SH*T

As you know by now, I like simple, common sense sayings that are memorable. This one is definitely direct, so please pardon my language. But I love it because it makes clear that every time you eat or drink something, you are making a choice. One path leads to feeling good, the other to feeling lousy.

Too many of us treat our possessions better than we do ourselves. If you had a collector car, say a Ferrari or a Porsche, would you service it with some lousy cheap oil? Of course not. Every oil change, you would get the best oil. Yet the same person who would do that often does not think twice before putting lousy food into *their very own body.*

I guarantee you the healthiest, fittest people on the planet have one thing in common: **they have good quality foods that they habitually eat, and they plan out what they are going to eat.**

There's so much advice out there on what to eat, both good and bad. It can be overwhelming. So to take away information overload, here are four simple principles to follow for a healthy diet:

1. When you feel hungry, eat more protein and/or fiber (fiber curbs appetite).

2. Keep healthy snacks at your fingertips. Berries, nuts, olives, and pickles are examples of good snacks. Low-sugar, high-protein snack bars are also a great option.

3. If you want to lose weight, reduce your carbs, sugar, and dairy. (I'm not saying to eliminate but at least reduce.) **Reducing calories consumed versus calories burned has worked for me for forty years.**

4. Learn to relax, eat your meals slower, and chew your food thoroughly. This will aid your digestion and allows for better absorption of nutrients.

Here are my other key recommendations to help you put healthy things in your body.

Always Have Water Close at Hand

Drink water all day instead of consuming sugary beverages of any kind. I keep my 26 oz. Yeti with a straw nearby all day long, which makes it easy to drink plenty of water. Good hydration helps keep inflammation down. And water can replace unhealthy drinks like sugary beverages, one of the biggest sources of empty calories on the planet.

This might sound like a small thing, but it is truly a key habit for health: have water next to you all the time and drink it regularly. **Astoundingly, up to 75 percent of Americans may suffer from chronic dehydration, which leads to fatigue, dizziness, and confusion.** Reference the water charts below to see how much you should be drinking daily and the importance of water to all of your body's vital organs. We personally use and recommend the Grander Energy Board to restructure our drinking water and increase the oxygen; once you drink it, you will never go back to regular tap water. For more information on structuring your water, go to www.vivacityimports.com (use code "TENACIOUS" for a 5 percent discount).

HOW MUCH WATER SHOULD YOU DRINK?

BODY WEIGHT	WATER INTAKE	8 oz. GLASSES
80 lb.	40 oz. / 1.2L	5
100 lb.	50 oz. / 1.5L	6
120 lb.	60 oz. / 1.8L	8
140 lb.	70 oz. / 2.1L	9
160 lb.	80 oz. / 2.4L	10
180 lb.	90 oz. / 2.7L	11
200 lb.	100 oz. / 3L	13
220 lb.	110 oz. / 3.3L	14
240 lb.	120 oz. / 3.5L	15
260 lb.	130 oz. / 3.8L	16
280 lb.	140 oz. / 4.1L	18
300 lb.	150 oz. / 4.4L	19

OUR BODY IS **70%** WATER

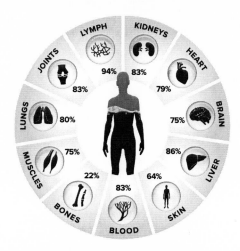

Cut Down on How Often You Eat

The science behind what is called **intermittent fasting** (IF) is growing every day. If you are not familiar with this concept yet, here it is in a nutshell.

Our bodies do better when they have a longer stretch without eating. One of the easier ways to start is to have a twelve-hour period without eating. If you stop eating by 8:00 p.m. each night and do not have breakfast until 8:00 a.m., you have that twelve-hour period covered. (You can and should drink water during your twelve-hour fasting time.)

There is another popular method that is a little more challenging and that is a sixteen-hour fast. With this, you stop eating by 8:00 p.m. every night, drink lots of water in the morning, and have lunch at noon. Have a healthy, filling lunch (you won't need as much to make you full when you fast for that long), and if necessary find a healthy snack during the day, before having a healthy and hearty dinner. Remember, no snacking after 8:00 p.m. and you are set for another fast until noon.

Intermittent Fasting is a well-researched way to keep blood sugar lower, help with weight loss, allow your cells to repair themselves, and give your digestive system a needed rest. **This is also a great hack for lowering your overall calorie consumption, which I will discuss in the next section.** If you want to go deeper into this subject, I would highly recommend the book by Dave Asprey titled *Fast This Way*.

(Being that I do not know the specifics of your medical history, I recommend speaking to your doctor or a nutritionist about any significant changes to your diet and your best fasting options.)

Calories In versus Calories Out Works!

Since this book is about tested habits and hacks, let me start by saying when I got married in 1991, I weighed 158 lbs, and my wife, Sally, was 125 lbs. As I write this book today, I weigh 150 lbs, and Sally weighs 118 lbs. The most I creeped up to was 165 lbs, and Sally was 130 lbs. Those were our top numbers and it told us it was time to hit the reset button and get back on track.

This is why I recommend everyone have a narrow weight range for yourself, and if you ever hit the top of that range, it is time to take action. This monitoring of our weight has allowed us to maintain our weight within a tight range for over thirty-one years consistently.

One of the keys is to count calories and put yourself on a stricter budget when you hit the top of your weight range. Counting calories sometimes gets a bad name, but it works.

I recommend using the Lose It app (explained in the next section).

I set my caloric intake around 1,500 calories per day based on my weight, and Sally is 1,200 calories per day based on her weight. Yes, we do have splurges from time to time;that is more of an exception not the rule. After just a little bit of time, you'll be in the habit of sticking to your calorie count and it won't require as much monitoring.

The bonus is that when you count calories, it also makes you read the labels of the foods you're eating. So when you check calories, also look at sugars, artificial sweeteners, fat, and so forth. This is also where reminding yourself that feeling fit is better than eating sh*t can be really helpful. To give you an example of what I mean, one Friday night I downed an entire pint of Baskin-Robbins Jamoca Almond Fudge ice cream. I looked at the container, which told me I just consumed 680 calories.

So the next day, I wanted to see how long it would take running at 6.5 mph on our treadmill to burn those 680 calories. It turned out to be one full hour of running at 6.5 mph. This is a clear example of why feeling fit is better than eating sh*t and a reminder that **you can't outrun a bad diet**. If I would have just skipped the ice cream, I would not have had to run an hour. I recommend using a fitness tracker so you can monitor calories burned and remind yourself of how your food choices impact how long and hard you have to exercise.

The Lose It App

One of the most studied and proven ways to eat healthier and lose weight (if that is one of your goals) is to track what you eat.

There are many apps out there that can help you do that. The one I recommend is the Lose It app, which you can easily search for in the Apple or Google Play stores. This is a simple way for you to track calories in. It also allows you to sync the app with a fitness tracker so you can monitor calories burned, too.

You can enter your goals, easily track what you are putting in your body, and get recommendations for healthier choices. Many of the diet and healthy eating plans urged on many websites, books, and television programs make things too complicated. Some are even good plans, but if they are too complex to stick with, how does that help you?

Simple is better because simple is more sustainable. Just commit to tracking your food and being guided to healthier choices by this app and you will get results. One of the ways the Lose It app makes things incredibly easy is that it is already loaded with an extensive library of foods. You can type just about any kind of food or brand name product and it will already have all the nutrition info and calories preloaded. In many cases, you can just scan the barcode of what you are about to eat.

The app also remembers your own previously entered food items, making it easy to track your regular foods without repetitively entering the same information again and again. It will even offer tips on what food items help keep you on track to your weight loss goal.

It's a great way to get visibility on how many calories you consume in a day. Some say significant calorie reduction can be dangerous, but I have found in my own life that it is beneficial. Be sure to run any significant dietary changes by your doctor.

We Eat What Is in Front of Us and Is Easy to Grab

Along these same lines of keeping it simple, here's another thing that is not exactly rocket science: **What you stock in plain sight in your refrigerator and pantry is what you end up eating!** Be mindful of what you are buying at the grocery store and cut out junk and stock healthy foods. If you do have some junk foods on hand, at least hide them in the back of the refrigerator or behind healthy items in your pantry or on a high shelf so they are not easy to access.

Too much common sense to ever work, right? Actually, I think it is brilliantly simple and effective. Every time you go to put something in your grocery cart, ask yourself, "Is this really what I want to be putting in my body?"

When you do fill your cart, here is what to put in it: **Focus on quality proteins and vegetables.** Reduce carbohydrates, especially processed snacks, breads, and frozen "heat and eat" meals.

Top Ten Amazing Foods to Add to Your Shopping Cart:

1. Eggs
2. Salmon
3. Pickles/olives
4. Blueberries or other berries (raspberries, blackberries, strawberries)
5. Sprouted almonds or other nuts (walnuts, pistachios, pecans)
6. Avocado
7. Broccoli

8. Hummus

9. Garlic and ginger

10. Spinach (leafy greens)

Even the Tooth Fairy Avoids Artificial Sweeteners

Too many people still believe that artificial sweeteners are like having your cake and eating it, too. Supposedly, it's a great deal because you get the sweetness of sugar without the calories. But the truth is, these artificial concoctions have terrible consequences, and they **can be as much as 200–600 times sweeter than natural sugar without your brain knowing the difference.** Below is a list of these sweeteners along with their alarming side effects. Cutting back on sugar is important, but cutting out artificial sweeteners is absolutely crucial.

Brand Names for Artificial Sweeteners (Avoid These):

- NutraSweet

- Sweet 'N Low

- Splenda

- Truvia

- Sunett

- Equal

- Nectresse

Side Effects of Artificial Sweeteners:

- Impacts your gut health leading to diabetes or gastrointestinal issues
- Weight gain from overeating (and some do have calories)
- Headaches or even migraines
- Depression and panic attacks
- They retrain your tastebuds, makes you accustomed to sweet food items
- Birth defects and infertility
- Allergic reactions
- Cell and nervous system damage
- Alzheimer's disease
- Brain inflammation
- Blurred vision and hearing loss

Your Brain Is Trainable

We tend to think that we are stuck with our tastes. We don't like broccoli; we do like Frosted Flakes. But you can override your brain's current opinion of a food.

Every time you eat a healthy food—especially vegetables and fruits—tell yourself how good it tastes. **Say it. Think it.** Associate healthy foods with other foods you do love and say you love it as much as you love that.

Of course, this will not happen overnight, and like I have stated before about changing habits or thinking, it could take months. But if you do this every time you eat it, your brain will learn to believe it. Sounds incredible, but it is true.

And remember, when all else fails, just fall back on my affirmation: **Feeling fit is better than eating sh*t! It will remind you that garbage in = garbage out.**

JUST GET MOVING; NO GYM REQUIRED

If you already have a regular habit of going to the gym, great. Keep it up.

But if you are not doing much exercise because you are waiting for your life to give you enough time to get to the gym regularly, then please STOP. Do not make it your goal to get to the gym every day.

Instead, keep it simple. Make it your goal to move every day.

Here's an example of what I mean. Could you do twenty push-ups today? Or if not all at once, could you do ten push-ups in the morning and ten in the evening? I am guessing that you can. Start with that, then. If you can't do ten, begin with whatever number you can, because it is the getting started that ultimately matters.

Do the math. If you do twenty push-ups a day for 365 days, that's **7,300 push-ups in a year.** Imagine the shape you would be in after 7,300 push-ups. And how easy it is to do twenty push-ups a day. Literally anyone has enough time for that. So start today. Right now is as good as anytime. Put a bookmark in the book and drop and give me twenty! I'll wait.

Good. Now do the same thing tomorrow. And the next day. And the next day. It really is that simple.

Keep at the push-ups every day for a week. Now add sit-ups,

jumping jacks, and standing leg squats. Do ten or more of each every day, morning and evening. You can do all that in two minutes or less. I know because I do this myself. I always listen to the Dazy Chain song "Level Up" while I do this two-minute routine of twenty-five reps of each of the four exercises mentioned above. This song is perfect because it is so upbeat and lasts exactly two minutes. If you want a visual demonstration, you can check out my video of my two-minute routine on www. tenaciousabundance.com.

At the risk of sounding a little bossy, I am going to give you a little tough love here for a second. If you are not already moving every day, what could possibly be your excuse for not adding this short, powerful routine into your day? Are you going to say you do not have two minutes to spare once or twice a day? Are you going to say that it is too demanding physically to move for a total of four minutes a day? Choose to be healthy, and start right here, right now. You have lost your last excuse.

Isometrics

Here is another type of exercise anyone has time for and can be done anywhere. Isometrics are basically holding a pose that keeps your muscles contracted for a short period of time. An example would be a plank position (which is like a push-up position, except your forearms are on the floor). You may end up being surprised by how holding a simple position for one minute can tax your muscles.

I recommend ten different poses, held for one minute each. In ten minutes, you will have had a solid muscle workout. **It requires no equipment, no complicated movements, and no having to remember a long routine.** There really is no barrier here except for a refusal to commit to ten minutes a day. (And to give credit where it is due, my wife and I learned about this routine from the program Longevity Blueprint, which was a program we found on the Mindvalley website.)

Please note, one minute each may be tougher than you think. If that is the case, simply cut it down to thirty seconds per position and work your way up to a full minute eventually.

Here are the ten exercises (a simple YouTube search will show you what each one looks like):

1. Standing squat hold

2. Standing bicep (also known as the gun show!)

3. Plank (push-up position only place your forearms on the floor versus your hands)

4. Superman pose (lying on your stomach with feet and hands in position of flying)

5. Reverse Superman pose (lying on your back with feet touching and off the floor while you crunch forward with your hands trying to touch your toes)

6. Squatting wall sit

7. Stand with your back against the wall and make fist and press against the wall at your side

8. Stand with your back against the wall and make a field goal signal, pressing the back of hands on the wall

9. Start a push-up but then hold it a few inches off the floor

10. Crunch hold or sit-up hold (this one is particularly challenging, so just go as long as you can and work up to longer times)

Weight Lifting Wonders

As we age, it is important to increase muscle mass, maintain bone density, and increase metabolism. All of this will lower your risk of injuries and falls, as well as boost your self-esteem and appearance. Weight training is one of the best ways to do all this. Isometrics are one way, but so are routines with free weights or selectorized machines.

If you do not have access to a gym, I recommend looking into PowerBlock dumbbells that allow you to change your dumbbell weight from five pounds up to sixty-five pounds, all in one unit. Dumbbells are great for your core, too, and there are so many exercises you can do with them, which you can find easily with a simple search on YouTube. Do not neglect weights for cardio. Do both, but if you have time for only one, I recommend isometrics and weights for aging well.

If you want to take this one step further, I would recommend purchasing a handheld dynamometer to measure your grip strength. Research has shown that grip strength can be related to and predictive of other health conditions, including osteoporosis, cardiovascular disease, cancer, and disability later in life. This simple tool can be the difference between predicting a future of thriving or premature death.

Sweat at Least Three to Four Days a Week

Even though I am very much an advocate that any kind of movement is better than no movement, you should set a goal to have a workout three to four times each week that is hard enough that you work up a sweat.

This will ensure you are getting sufficient cardiovascular exercise each week. Just as important, this will also ensure that your body is sweating out toxins, another key to maintaining excellent health.

Speaking of sweating out toxins, if you have the means, please look into purchasing an infrared heat sauna. Sauna bathing has existed for over 2,000 years, and during the 1980s, Germany and Japan introduced infrared heat saunas. Single units can range from around $500 up to $5,000 depending on the size. It's worth considering investing in one because the benefits are medically documented, including lowering blood pressure, improving circulation, ridding the body of toxins and metals, relieving stress, burning calories, and mimicking cardio workouts. I personally own a TheraSauna infrared heat sauna that has worked perfectly since it was purchased in 2006, so I believe in its quality and dependability. TheraSauna has patented infrared heaters and is the only company that is made 100 percent in the United States. (TheraSauna.com you can use the code "Tenacious" for a complimentary accessory kit.)

HUGE RESULTS WITHOUT EQUIPMENT

As you can tell from some of my examples above, you definitely do not need specialized fitness equipment to get moving and get healthier. Push-ups, crunches, jumping jacks, standing squats, isometric exercises, going for a walk or jog outside—the list could go on for quite a while. None of them require anything but you and your body.

Do not read this as me saying that buying a piece of equipment for exercise is always a bad idea. **The problem comes in when we think the purchase is going to do the hard work for us.** I know most of us would not put it this way, but I believe many people think their commitment will come from buying something, that it will somehow magically fuel a commitment to exercise regularly. A new treadmill will not get your butt out of bed for you, and you can walk, jog, or run without one.

Most of these purchases end up being used for a week or two, then they start collecting dust. Eventually, defeat is admitted and it gets put in a basement corner or gets posted for sale online. **Motivation and habits can only come from within!** The secret is not a piece of equipment; the key is to review your reasons for wanting to get healthy and work on your habit building. (See Chapter 5 for more inspiration in building daily habits.)

A good rule of thumb is to hold off on any big fitness equipment purchases until you have first built regular exercise habits that you stick to. Once you do that, then consider adding fitness equipment if it's still something you want.

HIIT AND TABATA FOR CARDIO TRAINING

For a fast, effective workout that will make you sweat and won't cost you a penny to do, try high-intensity interval training (HIIT). If you are new to this kind of training, search for videos on YouTube that are for "HIIT beginners."

The HIIT program my wife and I like best is either cycling or jogging at a comfortable pace for one minute thirty seconds, followed by a thirty-second intense cycle or sprint. We keep going through this alternating pattern, with a goal of completing a minimum of eight high-intensity cycles/peaks. However, we almost always end up doing extras because if you can do eight, you can surely do ten, and if you can do ten, you can do twelve, and so on. The idea is once you start and are already going, why not push yourself a little more.

There's also a version of HIIT that is called Tabata training. All of this is based on the idea of short bursts of output for twenty seconds followed by a short break of ten seconds and then repeated for a certain length of time. My wife and I enjoy multiple four-minute Tabata programs in broken-up sequences. Tabata is a little more advanced, so don't start with that if you have not done any cardio exercises in a while. But work up to it. We love training with Tabata routines on our cardio equipment, doing calisthenics, or watching YouTube videos. It is definitely exhausting but also fun, and you will feel great after you have accomplished a session.

BONUS HACKS AND HABITS FOR REGULAR EXERCISE

Tell Your Brain This Is Fun

Earlier in the chapter, I recommended retraining your brain to like healthy foods.

Do the same thing with exercise. Affirm to your brain that **movement is magical and working out is fun.** Tell yourself this before, during, and right after exercise. Here is a great affirmation to start with: **"The more I move, the better my mood."**

This is an even easier sell for your brain than changing your tastes, because exercise immediately does make you feel better and gives you more energy. Affirm it with your brain *consistently* and you will be amazed to find yourself looking forward to a workout.

Exercise Is a Reset Button and You'll Learn to Love It

Busy successful people often tell themselves they would love to take a break and get in a little physical activity around lunchtime, but there's simply too much work to do. This is backward thinking.

The truth is, exercise—the ten-minute isometric program, the two-minute level up, a simple break for push-ups, stationary leg squats in front of your computer, or a brisk walk after lunch—makes you more productive. It will more than make up for the time you spent doing the actual exercise by increasing blood flow and metabolism. It will be like a giant reset button, refreshing you for the rest of the day.

Do this a few days in a row and you'll start to wonder why you ever thought pushing through with no break to move your body was ever a good idea. Of course, you will still have to commit to it on your daily schedule or it won't become a habit. Why not just try it right now? Stand up and do twenty-five stationary squats and see if you don't feel more energetic afterward.

Do It in the Morning

Although a break in your day for movement is always a good idea, your main exercise should happen in the morning. Top performers know this and plan their exercise in the morning. It gets your day off to an energetic start and sets a tone for accomplishing your other priorities. **Exercising early has many benefits:** fewer distractions, avoiding the heat of the day, and it gives you better energy, focus, and mood during the day. And when you start your day with exercise, it helps you to make healthier food choices throughout the rest of your day.

Plus, I am sure you have experienced what happens when you put exercise off until the end of the day. It has happened to all of us. You'll often be too drained, or some obligation will pop up that will eat up your exercise time. Get it done first, and then you know it is done.

Music and Movement

With the right music, you either *forget* everything or you *remember* everything.

Using music for exercise has huge benefits. For one, you can use it to cue your habit that it is time to exercise. It can also keep you moving and inspired during the exercise itself and helps the time go by so much faster. Plus, it just makes everything more fun. Use the power of music to consciously build your exercise habit.

Music can also help you track how long you are exercising. Since most songs average about three minutes, I know that after listening to nine to ten songs, my thirty-minute workout is complete. Counting down songs is more exciting than counting down minutes.

There's more about the importance of music for the abundant life in Chapter 7 along with my list of workout songs as examples. Warning: listening to them will get you moving!

Buddy Up

When possible, have an exercise partner. A spouse and/or one of your children is ideal. Not only is it a way to spend more time with them, but it also creates accountability to each other.

If not family, I am sure you can be resourceful and reach out to others whom you could partner with. For example, find a neighbor willing to commit to a brisk walk together every day after work or a coworker who wants to buddy up during lunch to get moving. Another great option is finding a YouTube workout coach to follow regularly.

WELLNESS HABITS AND HACKS MOST DON'T CONSIDER

MINDSET MATTERS

The mind-body connection is real. Studies prove it, but I suspect you already know it's true without a study. Affirm for yourself on a regular basis that you treat causes, not symptoms.

Also, tell yourself that you "don't do sickness." Of course, this might not prevent everything, but the more positive you are, the healthier you will stay.

Of course, if you say, "I don't do sickness" but then constantly abuse your body with garbage food, rarely exercise, and run yourself down with a lack of sleep, this affirmation will do nothing for you. But if you both "talk the talk" and "walk the walk" this is an incredibly powerful combination.

BREATHE

Here's kind of a weird fact that should give us pause. Back in the 1920s, the average number of breaths most people took were about four to five per minute. Today, the average is an alarming eleven to fifteen breaths per minute. **So triple the breaths per minute from one hundred years ago.** We are under more stress now, and it shows up in our breathing, which becomes more shallow. The pace of our lives has made us forget how to breathe properly.

Here's what to do to start to restore some sanity to your breathing.

START WITH THE 4/7/8 BREATHING EXERCISE

Breathing to Relax
(4-7-8)

Inhale for a count of four.
Hold for a count of seven.
Exhale for a count of eight.

Adapted from Andrew Weil, MD

The easiest and most recognized breathing cycle is the 4/7/8 exercise. Sit quietly and relax. Inhale slowly through your nose for a count of four seconds, then hold your breath for a count of seven seconds, and last, exhale through your mouth for a count of eight seconds. If you follow this pattern, you are taking about one breath every twenty seconds. Do that two more times and you will have taken three breaths in a minute. You've really slowed down your breathing, which is very calming and beneficial to your health.

Purchasing a very inexpensive pulse oximeter can show your pulse rate and oxygen levels within seconds, something you should be aware of and tracking. (Later in this chapter under daily wellness ideas, there are also intermediate and advanced breathing techniques you can work up to.)

Practice this a couple of times a day—during quiet time in the morning and then again before bed. You are slowly training yourself to have better control of your breathing and to take deeper breaths. It is relaxing and increases your energy, your oxygen, and your focus.

I have been a big proponent of proper breathing for decades. Here's a little fun fact about that: I received the invention of the year award in Pennsylvania in 1998 for a handheld electronic breathing coach that I invented. With the help of Bucknell University's engineering department, they were able to build a working prototype. Tom Ridge, who would later go on to be the first head of Homeland Security for the nation, was at the time governor of Pennsylvania and gave me my award.

DON'T BE THE BIGGEST LOSER

Remember all the fuss around *The Biggest Loser*? That was the television show where people with extremely severe obesity problems competed to see who could lose the most weight. It was undeniably inspiring to see people lose all that weight.

But it was not real. The people did lose the weight—that part was true—but it was not the whole story. The truth is that most of the people on the show gained back all the weight and sometimes more. One of the hosts, Bob Harper, later gave an interview and confirmed that almost everyone gained it all back.

This is the problem with the "all or nothing" mindset. It's simply not sustainable. Forget too much, too fast. Forget absolutely killing yourself on cardio day after day. Just build habits slowly, be mindful of what you are putting in your body, and move every day. The tortoise wins the race, not the rabbit, so take it slow and then build up. **Remember, the idea is to become a person of health and fitness, not a workout beast.**

Create Good Sleep Habits

Restful sleep is crucial to good health; it restores your body and keeps you mentally sharper. But too many of us are all over the place with our sleep habits, me included. I have always had a hard time turning off my mind at night.

In Chapter 5, I share with you the end of my day and my sleep preparation routine in more detail. That routine is informed by these general principles that make for a truly restful night's sleep:

- Go to the bed at the same time every night and get up at the same time every morning (of course, there can always be exceptions based on a special event).

- End your day with calm and gratitude (more on gratitude in Chapter 8).

- No TV at least thirty minutes before bed. Have a few books on your nightstand instead. It's also a great time for breathing exercises to relax you or quality alone time with your significant other.

- Do not have your cell phone in reach from your bed. If you are concerned about needing it in an emergency, have it at least six feet from your body so you won't be tempted to use it for anything else. Also, have it completely off overnight, or at least facedown with all notifications off.

- Go for total darkness where you sleep; this includes all LED lights like on clocks, and other electronics.

- The best temperature for sleeping is between 65 and 69 degrees.

You should also not overlook the importance of your mattress and bedding. Being that most of us **spend at least eight hours (a third of our lives) in our beds,** you should consider getting that which most supports your health.

My wife and I purchased a Gold Organic Textile Standard (GOTS) mattress, pillows, and sheets to ensure we were not inhaling or absorbing any toxins from foam, glues, or chemicals from ordinary mattresses. You would be surprised how afford-able they are and the health benefits are enormous. We have tried many manufacturers and believe the best is Brentwood Home/Avocado mattress company.

Daily Wellness Time Ideas

In Chapter 5, I recommend creating a personal daily schedule, including building in time for daily wellness. This isn't to replace exercise or movement. The intent is to give you little islands of peace and wellness in your daily life and increase your overall feelings of well-being. Below are suggestions for actions you can implement during your own wellness time, separated out by experience level. Most of these wellness recommendations move your lymphatic system, strengthen your cells, and boost oxygen. These wellness ideas are built around improving your cellular health, **because healthy cells equals a healthy life.**

Beginner Wellness

(simple ideas + zero budget needed):

- Jumping jacks or jumping rope or jumping up and down for one minute

- Cold shower on forehead for twenty to thirty seconds everyday

- Walking barefoot to ground or sitting outdoors with feet touching the ground

- Sitting in the sun for at least ten to fifteen minutes each day

- Breathing 4/7/8 method (inhale for four seconds, hold for seven, and exhale for eight)

Intermediate Wellness

(some of these require a small investment):

- Mini-rebounder (We like Bellicon or Fit Bounce; they are quality rebounders)

- Cold shower on forehead for thirty seconds and then whole body for twenty to thirty seconds

- Grounding mat for under your desk by http://www.ulimatelongevity.com/tenacious

- Mini-lamp red-light therapy

- Navy SEAL box breathing technique (easy to find on Google or YouTube)

Advanced Wellness

(advanced techniques and/or higher budget required):

- Hypervibe whole-body vibration machine (use discount code "tenacious" for a 10 percent savings)

- Cryotherapy, cold plunge pool, or one-minute whole-body cold water in the shower

- PEMF machine (www.drpawluk.com is the country's expert in this space; check in the back of the book for PEMF product discount codes)

- Red-light therapy panels (We use platinum lights. A discount code is available at the back of the book)

- Wim Hof breathing method (www.wimhofmethod.com)

I would also remind you of the importance of having intimate time with your spouse. Besides the endless list of health benefits, it is easily the most fun of the wellness ideas. Of course, that is what I tell Sally every day (LOL).

Scraping the Tongue Morning and Night

Unless you are already familiar with this, it might sound like a strange habit, but it has definite benefits. Bacteria, dead cells, and other debris are always building up on your tongue. Removing bad bacteria helps keep your mouth and the rest of your body healthy. This has the added benefit of bad breath prevention and improves your sense of taste. It takes less than fifteen seconds, so there is no reason not to make this a daily habit.

It is easy to remember if you just keep a cereal spoon with your toothbrush and toothpaste. (By the way, antiseptic mouthwashes can destroy the good bacteria and nitric oxide in your mouth, so brushing your teeth and tongue scraping can be the better choices for oral health.)

Cold and Sore Throat Prevention

I don't do sickness, or at least it is extremely rare. I have had stretches as long as fourteen years without a full-blown cold or sore throat. If I feel even a hint of a scratchy throat or stuffy nose, here is what I do:

- I gargle with hydrogen peroxide for a few seconds and then spit it out. (Always be careful not to swallow it.) This works to get bad bacteria out of the throat.

- Then I do a NeilMed saline nasal wash—this is an easy-to-find nasal wash at your local grocery store or drugstore. This clears out my sinuses and helps prevent nasal infection.

- I consume hot liquids such as tea, coffee, or soup and also make sure I drink plenty of water.

I have found these steps to be completely effective in preventing me from getting sick. I don't take cold medication after getting a cold; that would be to treat symptoms. Instead, I go to the causes and flush them out of my body before they become a full-blown sickness.

Avoid Getting Trapped in Our Current Medical System

Let me start off by saying that there are many great doctors out there. I also believe in an annual visit to your doctor and doing recommended screenings for diseases.

But I also think our medical system is dysfunctional and it loves to treat symptoms and not dig deep to uncover the root causes. **This is in part because of profit motive; treating symptoms is more lucrative than simple preventive measures.** It's also more profitable to keep you on, say, blood pressure medicine than to help you reduce it naturally and get off the medicine.

You start to feel like a rat in a maze once the medical system has you in its clutches. Reflecting on this should give you powerful motivation to make healthy choices and lessen your chances of getting trapped in endless tests and treatments.

If you have a condition or disease that forces significant interactions with the healthcare industry, get advocates on your side. Find a friend or family member with experience in what you are suffering or with good knowledge of health matters and consult with them on what to ask and how to obtain useful information. It also is great if you have a spouse or close relative who can attend visits with you to ask great questions you may not think of on your own. **Having a "team" advocating for you is so important in these situations.**

Doctors deserve respect like all of us, but sometimes there is a tendency to grant them godlike status. They aren't gods; they make mistakes like the rest of us. It is also food for thought that pharmaceutical companies sponsor medical schools, medical supplies, and research. This leads to an inherent bias toward using prescription drugs for treatment and very little education about nutrition and wellness for doctors in training.

It is your body and your health, so don't be afraid to ask questions and always get second opinions with regard to surgeries, procedures, imaging, and labs that are for a serious health issue or carry a ridiculous price tag. There could be other options available.

Use PubMed.gov

There is so much health information floating out there on the web. Type whatever topic you are concerned about in an internet search engine and you will be flooded with an overwhelming amount of information. All sorts of "proof" will be presented with supposed studies.

You know the problem with this, of course. How do you know whom to trust? What studies can be relied on? My favorite resource for separating out solid information from bunk is the website PubMed.gov. This is the NIH's National Library of Medicine.

Only fully vetted, credible studies and information from doctors around the world make it onto this site. While navigating a family member's medical condition, some doctors told me about this site as the best source for medical and health information. I have used it ever since and I highly recommend it.

TARGETED SUPPLEMENTS AND PREVENTATIVE TESTING

As you can probably tell from this chapter, I dig into the details when it comes to healthy abundance and am tenacious about gathering the best information and testing it out in my own life.

So let me end this chapter with a handy reference guide for supplements and preventative testing. **I have highlighted what I feel are the most important supplements for each category.** (Supplements can get very expensive, so do not feel the need to start with them all.) You can waste a boatload of money on useless supplements, and I know this first hand because I have spent a lot of money testing them over thirty years. Use my guide below to choose the ones that have the most impact.

TARGETED SUPPLEMENTS

Heart Health

- **Krill oil** (smaller crustaceans contain less mercury)
- **Qunol CoQ10**
- Omega Q plus max
- Nitric oxide (Neo 40 or N101)
- L-Arginine

Brain Health

- **MCT oil**
- **B3 niacinamide**
- Phosphatidyl choline/serine
- CDP choline or citicoline
- Vinpocetine
- Lion's mane

Brain Performance

- **Adrafinil**
- **Modafinil/provigil** (take early morning or it can affect sleep)
- Piracetam
- Noopept

Gut Health

- **Fiber** (natural psyllium husk; Metamucil taste better but has sugars)
- **Apple cider vinegar**
- Bergamot (also good for lowering LDL in your cholesterol)
- Turmeric (also great for energy and reducing inflammation)
- MegasporeBiotic or Bio Schwartz Advanced Prebiotic

Sleep/Calming (Anti-anxiety)

- **Magnesium** (slow release)
- **Melatonin**
- Gaba
- L-Theanine
- Saffron

Energy

- **NMN or Berberine** (keep refrigerated)
- **Alpha lipoic acid or ALA**
- Acetyl carnitine
- Caffeine
- B12 methylcobalamin

Antioxidant

- **Glutathione**
- **D3 + K2**
- B17 or amygdalin (apricot seeds)
- Liposomal vitamin C
- Zinc
- Astragalus root extract (telomere health)

MOST EFFECTIVE PREVENTATIVE TESTING

Below are some of the most reliable and cutting-edge preventative tests available:

Heart

- CCTA or calcium score
- Echocardiogram
- Carotid artery ultrasound

Brain

- Amen Clinics—Brain SPECT

Cancer

- Galleri blood test (simple blood test for fifty cancers)
- Full-body MRI
- Colonoscopy/Cologuard

Mold and Mycotoxins

- Mymycolabs.com

Autoimmune

- Immunoscienceslab.com
- riordanclinic.org

Find Out your Biological Age

- biological-age.com

THE POWER OF 3s
CHAPTER SUMMARY

Top Ways to Implement the Concepts in This Chapter

Three Key Habits/Hacks

1. Drink plenty of water each day, especially upon rising (see chart in this chapter). I recommend using a twenty-six ounce Yeti with a straw to increase water consumption throughout the day. Also, scrape your tongue with a spoon upon rising and before bed at night.

2. Use the Lose It app to understand daily caloric intake; it will give insights on how many calories you should be eating each day. The most important thing is to choose quality whole foods, especially foods that are high in fiber. Stop eating after 8:00 p.m. until 8:00 a.m. (a twelve-hour fast is great for your digestive system).

3. Try to move every day, either exercise, walking, breathing, and/or my two-minute exercise or ten-minute isometrics. Get outside when possible to get sun on your skin and sweat out toxins.

Three Key Beliefs

1. Feeling fit is better than eating sh*t!

2. The more I move, the better my mood.

3. I treat the cause, not the symptom, and I don't do sickness.

Three Key Questions

1. What would be a healthier choice to eat today?

2. How could I make exercise more fun?

3. Who could I model that is leading a fit and healthy lifestyle?

CHAPTER 3

I AM WEALTHY

"True success is creating your own definition, then living it."
— Unknown

Becoming wealthy is way easier than most people think.

Shocked by that statement? I understand why people doubt it, but it is true.

First, please note that I did not claim that becoming wealthy doesn't require hard work. It does. And I did not say that there are not plenty of challenges along the way or that it doesn't take time. There are challenges and it does take time.

But it is still much easier than people think. It is a matter of knowing the principles that work for being successful in business and then making informed decisions to invest well. **There are certain strategies that just plain work and do not require luck.**

As you consider business and investment decisions, it is helpful to understand that large-scale economics have "seasons," just like spring, summer, fall, and winter.

I believe the US economy has been in a winter since 2008 and that it will last through 2027. You might question this since most people equate winter with hard times, but there are mild winters and severe winters.

I strongly believe we are heading into the worst part of this winter and that it could make business and especially investing quite a challenge. Our government debt is in the trillions, and derivatives are in the quadrillions. And our politicians talk about multibillion-dollar bailouts in casual ways, as if it is play money. It has me very worried about the next five years. **Just to give you some real perspective on how much a billion really is, keep this in mind:**

- A billion seconds ago, it was 1959.

- A billion minutes ago, Jesus was alive.

- A billion hours ago, our ancestors were living in the Stone Age.

- A billion days ago, no one walked on the earth on two feet.

- A billion dollars ago was only eight hours and twenty minutes, at the current rate of government spending.

To go deeper into this subject is outside the scope of this book, but if you want to explore the idea of seasons more, I highly recommend the book *The Fourth Turning* by William Strauss and Neil Howe. It goes into great detail about understanding and using seasons to your advantage.

Here is the good news: **no matter what season it is, there are certain evergreen principles that work in good times and bad**. It is my hope that by using my 7Ms to Success and

7 Wealth Tips, you will be armed with solid strategies that never go out of fashion.

WHETHER SUCCESSFUL OR NOT, EVERYONE NEEDS GROWTH

I love what I do as an independent fiduciary helping business owners control costs while also giving their employees needed benefits. One of the most enjoyable aspects is getting to interact with so many successful people.

Some are mega-wealthy, some are well-off, and some are on the path to get to one of those destinations. So if you are one of those who are already doing quite well, could this chapter hold any value for you?

I believe it will. Even the most successful people I meet are not typically using all of my 7Ms to Success, and anyone can up their game implementing all of them.

For example, one of the principles is modeling. This is where you look to someone already successfully operating at the next level and you model what they are doing to raise yourself up to that height. **And unless you're at the absolute top of your field, there is always someone at the next level you can learn from.**

That's this principle in action, and I believe no matter where you are now, you can benefit from implementing this principle. And business is more fun when you challenge yourself to up your game and increase your abundance right along with it.

The other place this chapter may hold value for you is with how you invest. I see entrepreneurs who are generating a lot of wealth and cash from their business who get investment advice that is either mediocre or downright lousy. It's painful to witness when you see someone getting less out of their money than they could.

That's why I have laid out the 7 Wealth Tips near the end of the chapter. Use them to guide you to the right strategies and the best advice possible. **Absolutely no one has a crystal ball, so the best you can do is follow proven principles.**

I have learned so much (and continue to learn) from other entrepreneurs, both clients and mentors. I hope that the accumulated wisdom here on both business principles and wealth tips can help you continue to tenaciously pursue abundance.

Let's begin with the principles of business and wealth, because first you need to generate money before you can invest it. Two quick notes before we dive into the principles themselves:

- These 7Ms to Success are personally tested. I have refined them over the years in starting many successful businesses across multiple industries (fitness, food, insurance, and financial).

- If your focus is not on starting a business but building a career, you can easily adapt all these principles with just a little thought. For example, on the first principle of motivation, instead of asking why you want to have a successful business, you adjust the question and ask why you want to have a great career.

GAME CHANGING: 7 Ms FOR SUCCESS IN BUSINESS

1. Motivation
2. Movement
3. Mentorship
4. Modeling
5. Manageable habits
6. Mastermind
7. Mastery

MOTIVATION

Always start with your why. **Seriously, do not pass go, do not collect $200, do not plan *anything* until you know your real why,** what is truly motivating you to desire running a business. (If your goal is not to start a business but to have a great career, you still need to figure out why—again, you just change the question slightly.)

I will warn you that digging for your why can get emotional, but don't shy away from that. It's how you'll know you are getting to the core. Let me share with you a simple but powerful way to get at your core motivation, and then I'll share a brief story of what happened when I did this exercise with a tough army ranger at Fort Benning.

Here's an Exercise for Finding Your Motivation

This is a written exercise, so grab a pen and paper to get started. Number 1 to 7.

Start by clearly stating your objective. Let's say your goal is "Open a business." Write this down next to number 7.

Ask "Why is that important to you?" Your answer might be, "So I can be my own boss." Be sure to write it down next to number 6.

Now ask, "Why is it important to be my own boss?" Maybe your answer is, "So I can control my future and make more money." Write that answer down next to number 5.

Then ask why it's important to you to control your future and make more money. Your answer could be, "Because my father got laid off when I was younger and our family struggled."

As you continue forward, you'll keep digging deeper and keep writing down your answers. Why is it important to you that what happened to your father does not happen to you? "Because I want the best for myself and my family and be able to be a steady provider." Why is it important that you be a steady provider? "So that my family can feel confident about their future and not worry like I did." As you drill down, the answers tend to get more emotional. Stick with it until you reach your deepest and truest why. (It's important to note that there is nothing magical about the seven blank spaces on the paper. You might get to your deepest why sooner than seven answers. It doesn't usually take more than seven, but the key is to get to your most fundamental answer, not to worry about how many answers it took to get there.)

Take your time with this exercise and be patient. When you've found it, hang on to that reason. Tape it somewhere visible and use it as a constant reminder to yourself as to your deepest motivation behind all your tasks, both the big ones and the mundane ones. Return to it when your motivation falters or when you're struggling to see the results of your work. When you hit that plateau and you're not sure where to go, come back and read your why again. It's surprisingly powerful.

This is the best exercise for discovering your true motivation. It has got to be something to get you jumping out of bed each day and fired up to make your business a success and for growing your wealth.

One memorable example of this exercise happened when I was doing a presentation on this topic at Fort Benning for the military. There was a top-ranking colonel in attendance that day. As I got to the PowerPoint slide about motivation, the colonel said, "Anthony, we want to send this out across American Forces Network (AFN), and we'd love to see you do this exercise with one of our audience members." Okay, so no pressure or anything! But when a top-ranking colonel gives you an order, you do it.

A big tough-looking army ranger was selected. I started to ask about his whys. As is typical, it started off with surface answers. But when we were getting down to about his fourth "Why is this important to you?" it did not feel like we were getting any deeper. I started sweating, hoping this wasn't going to fail in front of everyone. I was also hoping not to push this big guy too far and get my butt kicked.

Then on the fifth level of asking why it is important to him, he starts to get choked up. Turns out he grew up a blue-collar kid in Pennsylvania who had to overcome a lot of obstacles to become the accomplished and self-controlled person he was. He had a burning desire to do well in life. I asked him why it was important for him to do well in life.

He wanted to be all that for his family, to be a great example, and to be a rock for them. It was an emotional moment. This uncovered the motivation that he could now reflect on anytime he hit a challenge to remind him of why he was working hard. After the presentation, he sought me out and said that no one had ever taken him through an exercise like that and that it was so powerful.

Now it's your turn to get clear on your own motivation. Don't skip over this lightly. It's the foundation that will keep you steady through all the twists, turns, and challenges of launching a business or building a great career.

When discovering your deepest motivation, always keep in mind that you must find ways to add value to others. **Money is simply an echo of the value you create for others.** The more value that you create for others, the more success and money you will generate.

To give you an example, I'm sharing the results of my Why Exercise here. Remember to read backward starting at number 7:

"WHY EXERCISE"

1. Protect my family and ensure their future
2. So that my immediate family never struggles like my family did when my father died
3. Because no one showed my family how to do it
4. Ensure that their families are well taken care of
5. So that they have a sound financial plan
6. Help other people protect their families
7. Start Trupiano & Associates/Safe Money Solutions

One last thing about motivation. Too many people get stuck on how to do it or who can help them to get started in business. It's the what and the why that are clearly most important. **Know what you want and know why you want it first.** From there, you can figure out who can help and the strategy of how to get it done.

The right order is:

- What do you truly want?

- Why do you want it? (End goal is key here, not the means goal.)

- Who can help you or who can you model?

- Then the how (strategy) comes last; remember, there is always a way to get it done.

Over the past three decades, I have fallen into this trap of starting with the how and it never works. This is a common mistake, and when you make it, your plan will inevitably fall apart. So again, the order should be what, why, who, and then how. **Now go take action!**

MOVEMENT

As soon as you know your why, make it your goal to create movement. So many businesses never even get off the ground or flounder because people wring their hands, trying to anticipate and solve problems that haven't even happened. This is living in your fears.

And the solution is movement—take action! *Nothing* **will happen until you take action,** and momentum is so important to any business, especially one that is just getting off the ground. So no excuses; take at least one step each day. And always keep your action steps simple and easy to execute. Remember, one action each day is 365 actions in a year. That many actions will make a positive impact for anyone.

A question I hear frequently is why put movement as the number two principle? Wouldn't it make more sense to have it further down? It would seem to make sense to find a mentor first or figure out the business you will use for the modeling principle.

Although on the surface that makes sense, what I find is people who do not get in the habit of movement—taking action—always stay stuck in the planning gear. The greatest mentor in the world will not help you if you do not have a bias toward moving forward.

There's another reason movement must come early and often. If you go to find a mentor and you haven't taken the preliminary steps to launch, a good mentor will tell you point blank, "You're not ready." It's up to you to get the basics out of the way before reaching out, and that requires movement.

Let me give you a specific example. One of the most important mentors for my business has been Alan Meltzer, founder of the Meltzer Group, a hugely successful insurance consultancy. If I would have connected with Alan and said, "I'm thinking of getting in the insurance business," I have no doubt he would have told me to get back to him when I was properly licensed and in the insurance business.

Fortunately, I was licensed and in the business before approaching him. I had the movement before the mentorship, which is the right order. Figure out your true intentions and motivations, then create action, then find help to get to the next level. It always helps to take action in the proper order.

MENTORSHIP

Finding a mentor serves two purposes. It is a sure way of having support throughout your process, but it also can be someone who holds you accountable.

One key to approaching a potential mentor is to never ask for money or a job. Please recognize that super successful people get this all the time. It makes them understandably on guard and inclined to shy away from interacting with you.

Not to worry. Here is the magic key for unlocking a relationship with someone successful: **ask them to share their story of how they became successful.** I have done this many, many times with mega-successful people and I have never once had anyone turn me down.

All of us like to share our story. You will be pleasantly surprised by how much people will tell you. It is also a joy for your prospective mentor to realize you are not asking for money or a job and that you just want to connect with them, human to human.

Another key to finding the right mentor is to think like Goldilocks: do not aim too high and do not aim too low; go for "just right." An example might help make my meaning clear.

Let's say you're an agent at a huge financial and insurance services firm that serves people all over the United States. You're a relatively new agent who wants to find a mentor. Aiming too high, at least at first, would be trying to get the top agent in the country to mentor you.

Aiming too low would be looking for mentorship from a person in your office who is doing a little better than you but isn't knocking it out of the park. (Of course, you will still be open to learning from anyone who proves themselves to have something worth sharing!) For a mentor, though, it might make sense in this situation to reach out to the top agent in your local county or state. **Not too high, not too low. Just right.**

In general, look for someone who is killing it but not so many rungs above you that you may not yet be ready to implement what they teach you.

Here are a few more pieces of practical advice for getting a mentor:

- Identify what area of life you are looking for a mentor (could be business, financial, health, relationship, or spiritual).

- Determine what you are looking for in your mentor relationship. Are you asking for one-time advice or a long-term relationship? Do you want to model their business, or are you just looking for them to share resources that have helped them?

- Be prepared for meeting with your mentor with a list of great questions to ask, things like their why/motivation, who helped them, and how they did it. I also love asking what mistakes they made and how they learned from them. (Do not ask for money, a job, or an investment, and remember you are listening to their story, not telling them yours.)

- Be creative in contacting your potential mentor. Handwritten notes stand out; it is a great way to get someone's attention. I prefer to meet over meals because everyone needs to eat at some point in their day. (Be patient when waiting for a response; remember, successful people are very busy.)

- At the end of any meeting with a potential mentor, always ask what you can do for them. Also, find out what their favorite form of communication is (phone, text, email). But then do not blow up their phone with texts, calls, or emails. Remember to respect their time.

- Just be a great listener and just be yourself! Take notes and be sure to leave your meeting with at least three actionable steps to take.

I cannot overemphasize enough how life changing it can be to find the right mentor. In my business, that mentor was Alan Meltzer who I mentioned above. I would not have attained the level of success I have in insurance and investing without his generous and amazingly intelligent guidance. I wish for all my readers a mentor as wonderful as Alan has been to me and my family.

MODELING (AND NO, NOT THE KIND IN THE MOVIE *ZOOLANDER*)

This is one of the most overlooked principles of business success but also one of my favorites. In my experience, the shortest path to success is role modeling the success of others. Study what others have done to be successful in the same type of endeavor you are embarking on.

As Tony Robbins teaches, making money or having a successful business is a science, and there are many successful people who leave clues as to what you should do. Some are even willing to directly share their recipe with you.

Several years back, my wife and I bought a bagel franchise store from someone who was ready to get out of the business. Family members thought we were nuts. What did we know about the food service industry? They had a point about not being food service experts, but we had a practical solution. We were going to expand the offerings and create a better layout and operation.

Near us was one of the busiest Wawas in the country, a wildly successful convenience store chain. We visited the Wawa and it opened our eyes. How was everything set up? Where was the coffee? How did they use the placement of milk, eggs, and those kinds of products? We looked at everything and modeled our shop on that amazingly successful operation.

Here were the results of our modeling: we managed to triple sales within the first ten months and then sold the business for over double what we paid in 1.5 years. **People overlook the simplest strategies, when most of what you need to run a great business is an open secret sitting right in front of you.**

If it is a career you are after, then model someone in your industry. For example, do what the top salesperson is doing and follow their recipe for success.

MANAGEABLE HABITS (A.K.A. START SLOW AND REMEMBER THE TORTOISE WINS THE RACE)

Launching and managing the early growth of a business can feel overwhelming when looked at in the abstract. There is a lot to do, and then there are all the things you worry about that haven't happened yet. This type of mindset will have you chasing your tail and create exhaustion.

Stop trying to do so many things at once and focus your energy on a few simple steps each day. Write out your priorities for that day and then stick to them. **Getting clear on your top three items each day and getting them done first is the best way to stay on track without overwhelming yourself (more about this in Chapter 5).**

Also, if you are trying to get a new habit instilled that helps you as an entrepreneur, that's great. But again, keep it simple. A new habit won't happen in three weeks. It takes at least ninety days to start the rewiring process and then a good solid year to hardwire it into your brain and body. Another good reason to keep things simple.

MASTERMINDS (OR SIMILAR GROUPS)

I know you have heard it before: you become the sum of the five people you spend the most time with. It may have become a bit of a cliché, but it has a lot of truth in it. This is what makes mastermind groups so powerful.

An excellent mastermind will give you access to a lot of brain power, which benefits everyone in the group. It is a place where great questions get asked, and you can explore and bounce ideas off one another and get realistic feedback.

What's the best place to start to find a mastermind? Here are some proven ideas:

- You can begin with your industry association that matches your business. Joining that will give you access to some of the smartest and best people in your industry and also information about best practices and new technologies/products.

- Another great thing to do is to join or set up a local mastermind across industries. It could be based on serving a common target market. For instance, a financial advisor, an attorney, a CPA, and other similar professionals could form one. Finding top people is key, and as a bonus, you can refer each other.

- If you're a family-owned business, find several other successful family-owned businesses in your area that you don't compete with. Suggest getting together once a month for breakfast and talk about what you've been doing in your business and what's working well.

- If you are not a business owner, then just find other successful people who share your occupation. You can look within your own company, or other regions and states, or even other companies. Pick up the phone and give them a call or get on Zoom and talk each month about what is working and not working.

MASTERY (BECOME YODA OR BUST)

This last principle of business success is one that trips people up. Being human, we sometimes attain a certain level of success and then we let things get a little stale. Maybe we start telling ourselves a story about how we have hit our ceiling for growth, and we just start coasting.

But maybe you have more growth in you than you think. Return to the principles above. Can you find another mentor, one who has already taken it to the next level?

This is what the attitude of mastery is all about. **It is to continue to look for ways to grow, even after you have found some success.**

Here's the funny thing about mastery. Many people think it comes from knowing it all. Ironically, it's the opposite. When you train yourself to get your ego out of the way, that's when you become a master. When you are less worried about looking like the smartest person in the room, you become curious about what you need to learn to become better. **Curiosity trumps ego any day of the week.**

Mastery is not a destination; it is a never-ending process of striving for more knowledge and skill. (You can learn more about this in Chapter 4.)

Those are the 7 Ms of business success. Use them in the order presented and watch your odds of success skyrocket.

Remember also, if you are starting or growing a business, that amazing customer service has never gone out of style. **For thousands and thousands of years, it has been the foundation of any business: delivering value wrapped in great customer service.**

I hope that you follow all these 7Ms to Success and the wealth starts flowing into your bank account. But once it does, what do you do with it?

· · ·

As someone who helps people decide what to invest in for a living, I keep my finger on the pulse of the industry. And I can tell you, there are a lot of very smart people who generate lots of profit from their businesses or careers but then receive bland, unhelpful advice about investing or sometimes advice that is just plain misguided.

At the time of this writing, we are living through a historical bull market along with near-zero interest rates which has stumped even the best hedge funds on Wall Street. These are very difficult times to know where to invest. When you have the market manipulated by the Fed and top corporations buying back their own stock (thus diluting the true value), it can be tough to know where to turn. **In perplexing conditions, it can help to return to foundational concepts that never go out of style.**

SEVEN DIFFERENT WAYS TO THINK ABOUT WEALTH

THE MAGIC OF COMPOUND INVESTING

You must first find a way to produce a surplus of cash flow, after your living expenses and bills are paid. The standard advice is 10 percent, which is not a bad goal to start with.

However, it is also one-size-fits-all advice, and that is what I do not like about it. If you are just starting out, 10 percent may be too big of a struggle. Well, then, start with 3 percent or 5 percent. And then ratchet it up as soon as possible. You'll find that when you discipline yourself to save a portion right off the top, you do not miss it. The important part is to start.

Now that you are disciplined with creating a surplus, you must invest it and allow it to grow over time. This is where the magic of compound investing kicks in. **My favorite illustration about the power of compounding comes from a famous legend about rice and a chessboard.**

When the inventor of chess shared his game with the emperor of India, the emperor was so impressed by the new game that he told the man, "Name your reward."

The man said, "Oh, Emperor, my wishes are simple. I only wish for you to give me one grain of rice for the first square of the chessboard, two grains for the next square, four grains for the next, eight for the next, and so on for all sixty-four squares, with each square having double the number of grains as the square before."

The emperor readily agreed, amazed that the man had asked for such a small reward, or so he thought. After a week, the emperor realized that he was unable to fulfill his promise because by the sixty-fourth square, he would have to deliver more than 18,000,000,000,000,000,000 grains of rice, equal to about 210 billion tons.

This is the power of growing your wealth exponentially and why investing your 10 percent surplus can be so amazing.

Using a portion of these savings to put into a fixed product (like a fixed annuity) has proven to be a game changer for our clients over the past twenty-plus years. Some benefits: usually, fixed annuities do not have fees, the commission is paid by the insurance carrier, and the surrender charges mean most people will forgo the temptation to access the funds early. (The penalty acts as a strong incentive to force the savings.)

FIND A FIDUCIARY OR NEUTRAL PARTY THAT MUST SERVE YOUR BEST INTEREST

Of the people giving out investment advice in the United States, 90 percent are essentially salespeople, and the other 10 percent are fiduciaries. However, only 1.5 percent of those fiduciaries are truly independent and not working for a bank, brokerage, or insurance company. **A fiduciary is bound by law to put your interest first and also has to abide by disclosure policies that exceed the norm.** The fiduciaries that work for a bank, broker-age, or insurance carrier are answerable to their employers at the end of the day. Independent fiduciaries do not have those same competing interests.

For example, I mentioned annuities above. Typical advisors are not required to share what their commission is on a product, whereas a fiduciary is required by law to disclose that information. Not everyone understands why this is important to know, but it definitely is. Conflicts arise because some of the highest commission products have lower rates of returns or higher fees. **What is best for you is not always best for the advisor selling the product or service.**

The rule here is to do your due diligence and find someone credentialed and with a great track record who believes that full disclosure is important and must operate in your best interest.

IF YOU DO NOT UNDERSTAND WHAT YOU ARE INVESTING IN, THEN DON'T INVEST

Having a trusted advisor to help you is crucial. But that does not let you off the hook to understand the real cost of what you are investing in. Know all the fees and costs involved. I've noticed over my years of being a fiduciary that 90 percent of potential clients come to me and don't know the following about their investments: what they are paying as an advisor fee, the cost of their investments, how their current product is benefiting them, and how that product works.

An advisor with your best interests at heart will want you to know all this and make sure that you get all this information—you shouldn't have to even ask for it. Keeping your investments simple (like low-cost index funds) is a great place to start versus investing in expensive managed funds or retail funds.

Morningstar is a great service to help you. You can research investments and see what they rate as the best of the best compared to peer funds and benchmark indexes. At a glance, you can also get full disclosure, including fees, portfolio positions, and even commentary on management and category of each fund.

When discussing complicated investments with someone, if

you do not fully understand how it works, do not be embarrassed to ask for an explanation that makes sense to you. **Understanding what you are investing in and how it is beneficial to YOU is paramount, so either you understand it or you should walk away.**

THE MYSTERY OF ASYMMETRIC INVESTING EXPLAINED

Look for investments with more historical upside than downside, which is called asymmetric investing. For example, you need to be able to understand and compare an investment with a historic upside of 10 percent and a historic downside of −1 percent versus an investment with a historic upside of 20 percent and downside of −15 percent. A good advisor can help you make sense of this and make choices based on the strategy that best suits your purposes.

For the above example, many would just look at the upside of the 20 percent investment and not realize the risk of the possible downside of the −15 percent which equates to a possible historic return of only 5 percent. Although the 10 percent potential investment looks boring and less exciting, it actually provides better growth at a lower risk since it has a possible historic return of 9 percent. It's at least a factor you should always consider.

By contrast, most people just look at the performance of a fund and choose the one with the highest return. That's not enough, and it fails to take into account the power of asymmetric investing. Choosing funds simply based on the most recent performance is like looking in the rearview mirror to drive forward. You need to be looking out the windshield.

Most advisors will tell you that you need to take risks to beat inflation. However, more risk does not always mean more return;

sometimes it is just more risk and/or more fees. Keep in mind that the higher the fees you are paying, the more risk you are taking.

DIVERSIFY YOUR INVESTMENTS BASED ON SECTORS (OR WHY TO CONSIDER INVESTING IN POOP, WATER, FOOD, AND ENERGY)

Spreading your risk is a great principle. Most growth funds today are very unbalanced toward technology companies. A value fund has a more diversified group of companies in their index and therefore spreads risk better than most growth funds.

Also, make yourself aware of your investment funds top holdings. For example, if it is Tesla, be aware that they barely make money on cars or batteries or solar. Most of their cash flow is from selling carbon/energy credits. Be aware of how this may impact you! As my good friend Dr. David Martin would say, **investing in the fundamentals of civilized life (sanitation [poop], water, food, and energy) could be a good way to keep it simple, because without those, we have no civilization.**

It is worth emphasizing here again to invest in what you know and can understand, and don't invest in things you don't understand. **Sometimes the best investment could be in your own business or investing in education for yourself.**

CASH FLOW IS KING IN BUSINESS AND RETIREMENT

Most people understand that in business, cash flow is vital. It is also a crucial concept for your household during retirement.

This means you need to accumulate enough assets before retirement to have a good distribution of cash flow when you are retired. When you retire, whether selling your business or leaving your career, you must depend on what you have accumulated in savings, your business sale, or 401(k) plan.

This means you need to know what your lump-sum goal amount is to retire so you know what you are aiming at before you can retire. Base the lump-sum goal on earning a reasonable rate of return, plus factoring in your longevity. It is best to plan for an extended longevity so you won't run out of money in retirement. If you have an advisor, they could help you with these calculations. Or there are many calculators on the internet to help you figure out the lump sum required for your personal situation.

A good thing to remember is that you should run your retired life like a business. At its most basic level, you need to know what income is flowing into your bank account and what is leaving your account each month.

How will you take this lump sum and figure out how to make it last so that you continue to have sufficient cash flow throughout your retirement years? I am a fan of using a single premium immediate annuity (SPIA), which guarantees a cash flow to cover your monthly living expenses. This is the same way corporations pay out employee pensions, by using a SPIA with a top insurance carrier.

Since 30 to 40 percent of most retirees' income is from Social Security, you could just use a SPIA for the amount of monthly living expenses that Social Security does not cover. If you have extra funds after covering all of your monthly living expenses, then you could look to other investments for continued growth. **Understanding cash flow is more important than most realize.**

That is why you need a great advisor and CPA, which leads me to the last principle of wealth: having a team approach.

SURROUND YOURSELF WITH AN AMAZING TEAM OF PROFESSIONALS

Do your homework and find an exceptional CPA. That will pay for itself many, many times over. Tax codes are beyond ridiculous, and you must have a reputable CPA or CPA firm that helps you navigate this area. Combine a top-notch CPA with a great fiduciary advisor and an excellent lawyer, and you will have your team of professionals. It is like forming your own mini-mastermind group of professionals and keeps you on track to meet your wealth goals. Being self-employed for over thirty years, we have worked with a few CPA firms; however, Ed Lloyd & Associates is our current CPA and by far the best we have ever experienced, and they provide services nationwide, whether individual or business. You can contact them at tenacious@elcpa.com for interest in using their services.

A FEW FINAL THOUGHTS ON WEALTH AND ABUNDANCE

LIVE WITHIN YOUR MEANS

At first, it might seem out of place in a book dedicated to abundance to focus on limiting yourself, but you will never feel abundant if your motivation is trying to keep up with your neighbors or always spending to your limits and beyond.

Of course, you already know that living beyond your means will make you miserable, right? It's common sense.

But like I've already said a few times in this book, common sense is not common practice. It is easy to say, but many find it hard to resist overspending.

Sally and I used to live in a community where the homes were typically 5,000–10,000 square feet and with ridiculous taxes that couldn't be written off. Plus, there was the carry cost of a home (the amount it takes to maintain it).

This meant that many people ended up stretching well beyond their budget to buy and keep one of these homes. What was strange is sometimes Sally and I would be invited to our neighbors and we would enter to see only the sparsest of furnishings. They could barely afford the house, which left little margin to invest in the things that make a house feel like a home. I can't imagine they were able to invest toward retirement or many of the other things that life requires.

It was a little crazy to think about because these were houses that far exceeded the space requirements for the families that owned them, and they could have found a perfectly good house in a solid community for an affordable price. Instead, it seemed like they were living a high-wire act just to keep up appearances.

We ourselves downsized a few years ago, realizing that even if we could afford it, why not find something that fit our lifestyle (and of course, our yorkie's lifestyle).

There is always a balance between imagining a great future and living in your present reality. I would be the first one to say it is important to do things like investing in nice clothing for the appearance of dressing well.

And go ahead and visit the car dealership and sit in your dream car and smell the leather or to take a tour of a dream house. Visualizing success is so important (see Chapter 4 for more on this) along with actually seeing, smelling, and experiencing items that you have as goals to obtain.

But overcommitting and making purchases before you have the proper cash flow is a recipe for feeling miserable and anxious about your finances. **Dream big, but don't overspend before you get there.**

IT'S AN ACCUMULATION OF SMALL CHOICES

The final thought I want to leave you with in this chapter is that **becoming wealthy is an accumulation of small choices.** What prevents so many people from obtaining abundant wealth is a "play the lottery" mindset. Looking for a get-rich-quick scheme or thinking that maybe you will just get lucky and hit it big rarely works out. A better route is to find a great business and model your own business after it, building it up by daily action. Or if you are working hard in a career, take your surplus income and use the power of compound investing.

You should also be tenacious about the small daily choices that allow you to set aside money for savings and investments.

THE POWER OF 3s
CHAPTER SUMMARY

Top Ways to Implement the Concepts in This Chapter

Three Key Habits/Hacks

1. Find a true fiduciary advisor that by law must place your interest ahead of their own. If you don't do that, at least use a role model who has created the kind of results you want and then replicate what they do. Build a team of professionals around you.

2. Take a percentage of what you earn and place it in an investment with limited access so it can compound and grow over time (3 percent, 5 percent, or 10 percent, whatever you can do—just start). This habit will serve you well.

3. When starting and running a business or a new job, your deepest level must come before the how (strategy) of your business. Always start with why it is important to you.

Three Key Beliefs

1. Money is an echo of the value I create for others.

2. Where my focus goes, my energy flows.

3. Resources are limitless and always available to me.

Three Key Questions

1. Who could I model now that is getting the results I would like to achieve?

2. How could I create multiple sources of income in my life?

3. What one action could I take today to create more wealth or success in my life?

CHAPTER 4

I AM WISE

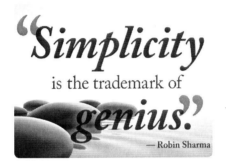

"*Simplicity*
is the trademark of
genius."
— Robin Sharma

A few years after World War II ended, the Americans in charge of Japan's postwar reconstruction were frustrated by the lack of progress in rebuilding the country's devastated economy.

Dr. W. Edwards Deming was at the time a well-regarded statistician and quality management expert in the United States, and he was asked to go to Japan to see if he could help rebuild Japanese businesses and to get their economy growing again.

Dr. Deming's impact was both immediate and long lasting. To this day, the Japanese honor his legacy with the annual Deming Award, presented to a company that has shown great improvement in productivity and quality management.

What was Deming's secret sauce? He called it total quality management (TQM), and it involved fourteen principles, plus a focus on measurable numbers and statistics. Whole books have been written about Deming's TQM, and a full analysis of it is well outside the scope of this book. But I bring up Deming's philosophy because one principle of it is highly relevant to this chapter.

One of the foundations of TQM is to be a little bit better today than you were yesterday. For example, you could aim to do something that improves the company's productivity by 1 percent. Then see if you can do something else tomorrow or next week that bumps it another 1 percent. **The accumulation of all these little improvements adds up to huge positive change over time.** Boiled down to its essence, the key to the philosophy is a commitment to constant and never-ending improvement, or CANI.

It's an incredibly powerful concept and not just for companies. This philosophy is also the key to growing your own personal knowledge and wisdom.

You already know that no one can become wise in one day. But what do you do with that insight?

- Are you going to commit to adding just a bit more knowledge and skill each day?

- Or are you going to just bump along, picking up a stray piece of information here and there but with no real strategy for how you improve?

Everyone knows that the first point is the best way, but very few people live it. By default, most use the second strategy of bumping along. That's a shame because improving a little bit at a time makes becoming wise fun and relatively painless.

It is far superior to a vague belief that somehow knowledge or wisdom will find you or that there is one magic piece of advice out there that by itself is going to make you instantly wise.

PAT RILEY USED 1% IMPROVEMENT TO WIN FOUR CHAMPIONSHIPS

In case you need more evidence of how powerful the concept of incremental improvement is, consider the strategy used by Pat Riley, one of the greatest NBA coaches of all time. He calculated his players' career best efforts (CBE) in all areas of the game (shooting, rebounding, assists, etc.) and then asked each player to improve at least 1 percent each season (not day or week or month). The results speak for themselves: four NBA championships and the fastest coach in NBA history to five hundred wins.

ARE YOU TRIPPING OVER YOUR OWN EGO?

In observing others over the years and in my own experience, there is one overriding factor in who grows in wisdom versus who stays stuck in a more limited perspective. That factor is ego.

People with big egos, who think that anything less than "knowing it all" is a sign of weakness, are never going to reach their knowledge and growth potential. I have no doubt that many of them will be able to maintain success and in some cases be able to fool others into believing they do know it all.

But ultimately, it is a miserable way to live, and in the end, it only costs them their potential for becoming abundantly wise.

Contrast this ego-driven approach with an attitude of humble curiosity. The most successful and intelligent people I have ever met are genuinely curious and never pretend to know more than they do.

The benefits of curiosity over ego can extend to every area of your life. For example, a huge part of my business is helping people and companies invest smarter. And what I have found is that in many cases, there is a herd mentality, even among knowledgeable and experienced investment consultants. "Everyone knows" thinking creeps in. But if you stay curious, listen more, you discover that what "everyone knows" often turns out to be false, or at least misleading. It's only by setting ego aside and being open to new ideas and trends that you can grow your knowledge.

PROBLEMS ARE A BLESSING

When you run into a problem or obstacle, get excited because that means you are going to learn something new. Jon Taffer from the popular television show *Bar Rescue* has created a famous saying that sums it up perfectly: **"I don't embrace problems; I embrace solutions."** Problems are possibly the best way on the planet to learn. When a problem arises, don't get negative. Adopt the mindset that you have just been given a gift and a chance to grow.

The key is to focus on finding a path to a solution. Here are five solution-oriented questions that have worked for me over the years:

1. How does this problem or obstacle benefit me and what can I learn from it that will help me in the future?

2. What haven't I tried yet that could help me? Take five to ten minutes to just brainstorm on ideas and write them out, then see if one or two items are worth trying.

3. Is there something simple I missed that I could try now?

4. What if I reverse engineer this problem and go to the end result and work my way backward?

5. Who can I ask for help that can shed some insight?

EAT AN ELEPHANT ONE BITE AT A TIME

Here is another great mindset for wisdom. Anytime you are using a resource for the purpose of learning, do not attempt to get every piece of wisdom out of it. Pick one thing and impress it upon your mind, and then ask what action you can take to make it practical in your own life.

Examples:

- When you read a book at night, stick with a few pages at a time or single chapters, and truly reflect on it. A great hack is using www.blinkist.com for a 15 minute synapsis of over 5,000 books with key points to read or listen to.

- When you listen to a fifteen- to thirty-minute YouTube video, do not try to fully grasp every point. Instead, choose the one thing that sticks out to you. How can you apply it to your own life?

- If you attend a seminar or listen to a webinar, do not put pressure on yourself to gather in every nugget. Pick the top three insights that most stood out for you and implement them.

Too many times, we think we have to squeeze every bit of knowledge out of a resource to get the value out of it. That's a recipe for getting less value out of it, not more. If a resource truly has that much value, then do not try to get all of it at once. Instead, return to it again and again, each time slowly taking in more. That is a better way to make it stick.

(I can be just as bad as anyone about this! I laugh at myself sometimes, having returned from many seminars with more notes, manuals, and ideas than anyone could implement in a lifetime. I so rarely go back through all that material; the paper would have been better used as kindling than as notes. This is why pulling out a few simple ideas is always better than trying to capture every single concept.)

A TENACIOUS SEARCH FOR WISDOM

As I mentioned in the Introduction, I have spent more than three decades attending seminars, workshops, reading books, listening to audio courses, and consuming every other resource you can think of from the best in the world. In this next section, I would like to share with you some of the wisest strategies, mindsets, and habits I have learned.

HABITS AND PROCESS ARE THE KEY TO SUSTAINED ABUNDANCE

If you are reading this book straight through, you have probably noticed a theme. **Small daily good choices repeated consistently will always beat some over-the-top one-time effort.** If you are tenacious in pursuit of good daily choices, abundance will follow. The huge one-off effort rarely leads to any kind of sustained abundance.

If you struggle with creating habits, I highly recommend you read the next chapter about making a personal daily schedule. If you do not create your own days, you will never make progress that lasts. Another great resource in this area is the book *Atomic Habits* by James Clear, the modern-day master of habits. I strongly recommend the book as well as his weekly email newsletter which is very short and to the point and free.

ATTACKING YOUR HARDEST TASK FIRST

Do you want to be more productive and set the tone for a happy day? **There is no better piece of wisdom for this than to set your priorities for your day and then do the hardest one first.**

Training yourself to do your hardest task first every day is like building a muscle. It is crucial that you exercise that "muscle" every day until it is a strong habit. Once you do that, it is life changing. There is no better hack in this chapter than this one. Working on the hardest priority item first each day sets you up for immediate success.

In Chapter 5, you can read a more detailed recommendation for implementing this in a section called "3 Anchors." Read it. Take action. Watch your life change.

Always Add Value

In the book's Introduction, I introduced one of the wisest things my dad ever told me. In case you are the kind of reader who skips introductions, I want to make sure to share it again here. He said:

"There are two types of people in the world. There are people who add value and people who take away value. Always be the person that adds value, and you will have a great life!"

Simple, right? But this is one of the most important filters you can use for every action you take in life. **Are you doing something that adds value to others, or are you wasting time and energy on trivial concerns that do nothing for you or anyone else?**

Are you more worried about what you are taking out of a relationship than what you are adding to it? Then you have lost your way, and true and fulfilling abundance will be beyond your grasp. Time to hit the reset button and give more value than you get.

Do not complicate this advice. Ask questions like:

- Am I adding value right now?

- How could I add more value for my customers, clients, family, friendships, and community?

- Am I sincere in wanting to add value to others, or is my primary concern what I get out of it? Long-term abundance is fueled by truly wanting to provide value to others.

- Remind yourself that money is an echo of the value we create for others.

Asymmetric Decision Making

Here is one of my favorite frameworks because it brings remarkable clarity to any decision you're considering. It's particularly valuable for motivating action when you think something sounds unlikely but could have a huge payoff.

First, let's define **how asymmetric decision making (ADM) works,** and then I'll give you some specific examples so you can see for yourself just how powerful it is.

Step one of ADM is assessing the potential upside and the potential downside of any action you're contemplating. Step two is to take those assessments and compare them for risk and reward.

If the potential downside is small and the potential upside is great, that's very asymmetric in your favor. That tells you the decision to take action is a no-brainer. Why would you not do something that has very little risk but potentially has a tremendous payoff?

Now let's look at some examples of how this might work in the real world. One of my favorite ways to use this framework is for deciding to reach out to someone who you don't think will respond.

Let's say you have a son who is a high school quarterback. You know it would be a tremendous boost to him if he could get a little time with an elite pro quarterback to get some advice and inspiration. Possibly, it could be an actual meet-up at a field or maybe just a phone call or personal note. Either way, it would be a huge win.

So who is the most elite quarterback you can think of? Tom Brady? Peyton Manning? Patrick Mahomes? (Or maybe you choose the starting NFL quarterback closest to where you live.) I know your mind is immediately rebelling and you're thinking, "Not going to happen."

Instead of that knee-jerk reaction, put this idea through the ADM framework.

What does it cost you in time, effort, and risk? The time and effort would be small. You'd need to think about various ways to reach out (phone, personal handwritten note) and then research how to get the number or address. Maybe a little time figuring out if there is a representative to go through to best reach that person. And then the time to make that call or write that note. That's it.

Now, what's the risk? It's zero. Z-E-R-O. The worst that can happen is you're ignored or the person tells you no.

Let's look at the other side of the equation. What's the potential upside? It's gigantic. Even a brief phone call with some advice from Tom Brady would send your kid over the moon and give him some valuable insight on success on the field.

The asymmetry of risk here is off the charts in favor of taking action. That's how ADM works. I should add that if you think that this sounds like an outlandish example, it's not. You'd be shocked at the number of supposedly unreachable people who will give you a positive response. The key is to not go in asking them for money, a job, or anything like that.

Ask them for their story and their advice. Show them that you sincerely want to learn from them. **Successful people love to share their stories and truly want to help.** I can tell you from experience that if you can break through and reach a person, they will not refuse as long as you approach them this way. You can use it on hiring an employee, cost versus production increase, or maybe making an equipment purchase for your company; the uses are endless.

How I Met a Legend Using ADM

If you are still a little skeptical, let me tell you how I met the greatest basketball coach of all time, John Wooden, and even spent an afternoon visiting him at his home.

Originally, I had no intention of meeting any basketball coach, let alone a legend. I was actually trying to do business with an NFL football coach. I lived near Jacksonville, Florida, and the hometown football team is the Jacksonville Jaguars.

At the time, the Jaguars head coach was Tom Coughlin. I wanted to give a seminar for the Jaguars coaches on success principles. Through a connection, I was able to get a meeting with Coach Coughlin, but it was not going well. He is not the warmest of personalities, and I was struggling to make a connection.

As I looked around his office, I noticed he had John Wooden's book on his shelf. For those unfamiliar with Coach Wooden, he was the basketball coach at UCLA from 1959 to 1975, winning an astounding ten NCAA championships. In four of those seasons, his teams went 30–0. So yes, I think it is safe to call him the greatest basketball coach of all time.

"I see you're a fan of Coach Wooden. I'm a fan of his, too—I've read all his books," I said to Coach Coughlin. I asked if he had ever spoken or met him, and he said no.

"Why don't you call him?" I suggested. "You're an NFL coach; I'm sure he would respond."

Coach Coughlin rejected the idea that he could just reach out to John Wooden. So I said, "If I could get him to call you, would you be willing to go forward with my presentation to you and your coaching staff?"

Coach Coughlin was a bit dismissive about my chances of

pulling it off, but he agreed. When I got home from the Jaguar stadium that afternoon and told my wife what happened, even she thought I was off my rocker. "You don't know John Wooden!" It was a fair point for her to make.

But logically, I thought it could very likely work. You have two big-time coaches; why could they not connect? I wasn't asking for him to call a random person. Besides, I was using the ADM tool. What did I have to lose? I found contact information and picked up the phone and reached Coach Wooden's assistant.

I explained that NFL coach Tom Coughlin was a fan and would love to hear from one of his coaching heroes, John Wooden. At about eight o'clock that night, the phone rang and Sally answered. She had a look of amazement on her face as she handed me the phone. "It's Coach Wooden for you."

Happy as I was to hear from him, I thought maybe there was some confusion. I explained that I had been calling for him to reach out to Coach Coughlin.

"I know. But the person I am more interested in talking to is the young man who reached out to make this happen," Coach Wooden said. Ironically, I would go on to talk a few times by phone with him and even was invited to visit with him at his home for a day.

I will tell you it was gratifying to find out that Coach Wooden's private personality matched his sterling public reputation. He was a very gracious host to me when I visited. I think he could best be described as a caring teacher, and there was not even a hint of insincerity in how he conducted himself.

Coach Wooden was known for a coaching philosophy of

being methodical and precise in practice and preparation. Games are won before they are played by disciplining yourself to always do things the right way and not take shortcuts. This applied for everything from how you wore your socks and tied your shoes to how you played team defense.

Essentially, Coach Wooden was the expert on creating the right daily habits for success well ahead of his time. I remained in touch with him up until his passing in 2010. I cherished the time with him, and it all started because I was not afraid to just reach out to him.

By the way, Coach Coughlin did speak with Coach Wooden, and I was hired to work with Coach Coughlin and his entire coaching staff at the Jacksonville Jaguars. These strategies work!

"IMAGINATION IS MORE IMPORTANT THAN KNOWLEDGE"

This famous quote by Albert Einstein is one of my favorites. Imagining something for ourselves is what motivates us to learn more about how to get it. When you can put yourself in an imagined future of abundance, it drives you to more knowledge and wisdom because you say, "Okay, but how do I get to my vision from here?"

There is also something powerful about imagination that gives us more confidence and tenacity to move boldly toward what we want. This is one of the reasons I use a vision board, which I update annually based on my latest goals. Here is my most recent version that you can use as an example. I used Canva to create my board; however, you could also simply cut out pictures and place them on a poster board.

(By the way, if you look closely, you'll see that you are reading this book because it was on my vision board for 2022!)

I strongly recommend you create your own vision board and place it someplace where you see it frequently every day. **It will work its way deep into your imagination and keep you focused on what matters most to you.**

You'll notice mine contains my most important affirmations, monetary goals, supportive statements for a healthy life, and a reminder to give back. Customize your own using similar principles and ideas.

One piece of advice: Aim high, but keep it realistic. If your current net worth is $200,000, perhaps don't make your five-year goal to exceed the net worth of Warren Buffet. Set an amazing goal for yourself, but do not make it crazy. Once you hit that goal, then ratchet it up again on your next vision board. **Remember, logic will take you from point A to point B, but imagination will take you anywhere you wish to go.**

Tell Yourself What You Want

Here is a short but important story that illustrates the power of being very concrete about what you want. In 1999, we had just sold a food business after tripling sales in ten months and selling it for over double what we had paid a year and a half prior.

It was a great success, but I also learned from the experience that I did not ever want to be in the food business again. We lived in Pennsylvania at the time, and I went to the basement of our home and turned on music from the *Braveheart* soundtrack and wrote out how I would like our lives to be.

I said we wanted to live in a warm climate where the sun was out most of the time and the people are friendly. I wanted to drive a sporty car like an Audi TT, and I wanted to return to a job where I got dressed up in suits to go to work. I also wanted to get back into something that revolved around my love for financial and insurance products.

The very next year (2000), we moved to Florida and I drove down in an Audi TT, with my newly purchased suits ready to unpack. In 2001, I earned my insurance license for Florida and launched Trupiano & Associates. Everything I wanted came true in a very short time after being specific about what I wanted.

It's now over twenty-one years later, and my family and I have never looked back.

Visualization Insights

This is based on the same principle as the vision board. **What you imagine, you move naturally toward.** So find some quiet time, lie down, close your eyes, and visualize whatever it is you want to accomplish.

It is vital to set a target for your subconscious that is easily in sight each day. Your **reticular activating system** (RAS) needs a target to view daily; that is why focusing on a vision board works.

To give a simple example of how your RAS works, you may remember when you were a child playing a game while traveling called the punch buggy game. The idea was to see how many Volkswagen Bugs you could spot before someone else in your car did. The winner was the one who spotted the most VW Bugs before arriving at the destination. (In some versions of the game, you lightly punched your brother or sister in the back seat each time you spotted one, but we'll stick with the nonviolent version.)

Your vision became very attuned to VW Bugs, and all other cars—Cadillacs, Porsches, and so forth—faded into the background and were just not noticed. Simply put, what you look for and focus on, you will find.

So make sure you place your vision board where you see it all the time, like your office, on your computer background, or even taped to your bathroom mirror. The more you can remind yourself of your most important goals, the better chance you will have of achieving them. **Be sure to also take one action a day toward each item or even just one item on your vision board and magic will happen.**

Earlier, I shared that because of a loan from a kind neighbor when I was in high school, I was able to attend the best wrestling camp in the country one summer. While at that camp, at the end of each day, the coaches had us all lie down on the mat, close our eyes, and imagine wrestling our very best and winning. This is a technique that I have been able to use my whole life to increase my chances for success. Imagination is an amazingly powerful tool.

The Best of the Best for Motivation

I am sometimes asked for the best resources for staying tenacious and motivated about gaining wisdom. Here are my top five resources for motivation and wisdom; they never let me down. (And all but the first one are free!)

1. Mindvalley programs
   (a personal growth learning platform, membership
   required. You can find it at mindvalley.com)

2. The Tony Robbins YouTube channel

3. Ed Mylett's podcasts
   (see Chapter 6 for more info)

4. Evan Carmichael's top ten
   (see Chapter 6 for more info)

5. James Clear's 3-2-1 Thursday Newsletter
   (sign up at JamesClear.com)

6. www.blinkist.com over 5,000 books with
   15 minute audio or key concepts

Relationship Wisdom

I have been happily married since May 1991 or for more than
thirty-one years at the time of writing this book. I am the first to
admit that I married way over my head. (I think the only thing
that gave me a shot was my infectious sense of humor!) However, a good marriage isn't pure luck. Investing time and care in
your relationship makes all the difference.

My wife and I share our priorities and beliefs and that main-
tains harmony. When you have consistent arguments with a
spouse, it is almost always because you have different perspec-
tives or beliefs about an important topic.

Here is what I recommend if you are having conflict. **Each
spouse spend some time writing down their top three beliefs
about:**

- Money
- Raising kids
- Expectations from spouse
- What makes for a happy life

Then set aside some time to come together and discuss your answers. **I guarantee you will learn things from each other that you had no idea about.** If you truly listen, you will also find ways to make your spouse happier. This would also be a great exercise for a couple considering marriage as well. The hope is that there are some common beliefs to agree on. At the very least, you both will know where you stand in these areas. (This could also be a valuable tool for hiring a new employee or working with a business partner. Find out the top three beliefs in different areas of the business or job duties.)

Above all, commit to honesty first and foremost. **Remember, you only have to tell the truth once, but if you lie, then you must continue lying to cover the initial lie.**

THE POWER OF CONSTANT AND NEVER-ENDING IMPROVEMENT

There are very few things in life as gratifying as learning something new and then improving your life with it and also the pleasure of sharing it with family and friends. Keep improving a little at a time using the advice in this chapter and see your abundance grow. I learned many decades back the power of constant and never-ending improvement (CANI). **The CANI attitude will change your life.**

THE POWER OF 3s
CHAPTER SUMMARY

Top Ways to Implement the Concepts in This Chapter

Three Key Habits/Hacks

1. Do your most important or hardest task of the day first. I promise you, this will change your life. Keep your vision board in sight, too.

2. Keep a book on your nightstand and read at least a page or two each night, which creates the habit of becoming a reader. Or listen to a podcast every night to become a learner.

3. Join a program like MindValley where you can have access to some of the most successful people at a very reasonable cost. Most of their programs are broken out into small time frames each day, so they are very simple to fit into your daily life. There are other amazing resources you can benefit from like Ed Mylett podcasts, James Clear's weekly newsletter or blinklist for a synapsis of over 5,000 books.

Three Key Beliefs

1. Great habits = Great life.

2. I always have time for what is most important.

3. Simplicity is the trademark of genius, so keep it simple.

Three Key Questions

1. How can I make learning something new both simple and fun?

2. Who could I model knowing the shortest path to success is finding a role model?

3. In what ways would my life improve by learning something new each day?

CHAPTER 5

CREATE THE PERFECT DAY, THEN LIVE YOUR PERFECT LIFE

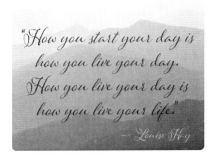

"How you start your day is how you live your day. How you live your day is how you live your life."
— Louise Hay

Are you a firefighter? Or are you a creator?

When it comes to how we manage our individual days, we tend to fall into one of these two types.

If you spend your days mostly *reacting* to whatever the day throws at you, you are a firefighter, spending most of your time putting out whatever "fires" the workday brings you. People who fall into this category tend to show up and work on whatever is in the piles on their desk and then wait to react to whatever problem walks through their door that day.

Firefighter types often continue this same pattern in their personal lives. Maybe you get up just in time to wolf down a breakfast, get family members where they need to be, and then it is off to work. In the evening, you are often exhausted from reacting to fires all day long. Perhaps you have the energy for a bowl of ice cream and zoning out with the television before going to bed too late, only to get up and do that same Groundhog Day all over again.

If any of that sounds even a little familiar, you are probably a firefighter. Don't beat yourself up, but please also recognize that you will never get consistent abundance in your life with this mindset. (Needless to say, I'm not talking about real firefighters here! They have my gratitude for putting out real fires and often being the first response to other difficult situations.)

There is another (and far superior) way to manage your days, and that is as a creator.

THE KEY TO SUSTAINED ABUNDANCE: YOUR PERSONAL DAILY SCHEDULE

Believe me, I am not judging anyone who has struggles staying in charge of their day, particularly business owners or parents with children, especially single-parent households. I have the utmost respect and admiration for businesses that produce real benefits and deliver value to their customers, their employees, and their communities, and for parents trying to raise kids in these very crazy times. It is an extremely busy life, and I know that everyone seems to come to you for answers without regard to how it impacts your schedule.

But this is exactly why you need the information in this chapter. *You* **have to decide if you are the boss of your own day,** or if you are going to allow other people and circumstances to be in charge of it. **How you spend your day is** *a decision.* You have to decide to create your own day.

Even not making a decision to control your daily schedule is a decision. It's a choice for a chaotic day based on the whims of others and outward circumstances. **Most of us live our days on autopilot without realizing what habits or schedules are running us.**

Let me acknowledge something else up front. There will be days where you do have to be a firefighter. If one of my daughters called me in the middle of any day and said, "Dad, I had an accident. Can you come get me?" I have a new immediate priority. I'm sure you can think of other scenarios, both personal and work, that would justify other legitimate reasons for your day to go sideways.

If getting complete control of creating your day sounds daunting, here is good news: there's a way to make great strides immediately. **The secret is to use anchors.**

ANCHORS AWAY TO START AND END YOUR DAY

This chapter is packed with details on creating an optimal daily schedule, but to begin, let's go directly to the heart of the matter. If you master the **3 Anchors Method** that I'm about to share, it will change your life. What's amazing is this: not only is it powerful, but it's also incredibly easy to implement.

There's literally no good excuse for not doing it. You could start doing it tomorrow and just never stop.

Here it is in a nutshell: to be in control of your own schedule, you need to have three anchors every day.

- **Anchor #1:** Plan when and how you'll start your day and then do it.

- **Anchor #2:** Write down and complete your top three priorities for the day.

- **Anchor #3:** Plan when and how you'll end your day and then do it.

STARTING YOUR DAY

No matter how busy you are with work, family, or other obligations, you can and should have a plan to start your day. If you have a time crunch at the beginning of your day, start getting up thirty minutes earlier. Whatever you need to do to block off some quiet time at the beginning of the day, do it.

Later in this chapter, I'll give you more strategies and ideas in setting up an optimal early morning. But for now, I only want you to set aside at least thirty minutes (work up to forty-five to sixty minutes) to do the following three things.

Write in a journal a list of at least five things you are grateful for and/or blessings that have recently come to you. Next, spend a few minutes meditating or praying and do your affirmations. Finally, write down that day's top three priorities (see the next step).

Your Day's Priorities

When selecting the day's priorities, stay focused on only the most important, high-leverage things you can do for your business or career that day. If you have a list of ten things, that's way too many. I find that three priorities are often optimal, but some days you may have only one or two. **Intention matters here, so be crystal clear on your intent.**

If you have something that you're working toward that can't be accomplished in a day, then break it down into one bite-size piece that you can realistically complete on that day. You want your priorities to be something you can point to and say that it got accomplished today and makes you feel the day was successful.

There are two keys to executing on your top priorities. One, always do the hardest ones on the list first. Two, complete all your priorities as early in your workday as you can. There is no better feeling than knocking out the important things in your day first. You'll also be amazed by how much more you start getting done.

The End of Your Day

A great end to your day starts with having a planned bedtime, one that is early enough to get you the sleep you need and wake up truly rested.

Use the thirty minutes before bedtime to transition from the noise of the day to the peace of sleep. No television, social media, smartphones, or computers during this half hour. Have a book on your bed stand and dip into it for some wisdom or use this time for breathing exercises that relax you. Quality alone time with your significant other is also important.

If you have a spouse, share positive things that happened that day and enjoy each other's company. Jot down what you have gratitude for from the day. It's these simple acts that remind you of what's important and clear any daily stress from your system.

Park your phone away from the bed. I recommend creating a bedroom of total darkness for the best sleep conditions. Select a meditation to play as you go to sleep. If you still have trouble gearing down, try a few cycles of the 4/7/8 breathing technique (how to do this breathing exercise is explained in Chapter 2).

WHY THE 3 ANCHORS ARE LIFE CHANGING— PERIOD

The bottom line is, you can't change your life if you don't have control of your daily schedule. Without an intentional schedule, you're stuck in an endless loop of reacting to your day instead of creating it, and no progress can be made.

This is why I love the 3 Anchors Method and believe it to be the key to transformation. If you're new to taking command of your day, this gives you a simple and completely attainable way to get started. You'll immediately see the benefits—it's that powerful. Once you master it, you can go on and implement a more detailed daily schedule.

I also love it because it will be something you can return to again and again, even as you get better at controlling the rest of your day. If you have a bad day or start slipping away from creating a daily schedule, go back to basics with the three anchors. You'll get back on track.

If you have one of those days that ends up full of surprises or an emergency, your three anchors will still allow you to have a good and productive day. The three anchors are the core; implement this strategy and watch your life radically improve.

MY PERSONAL DAILY SCHEDULE (BE A COPYCAT; IT'S OKAY)

Using the 3 Anchors Method is a beautiful way to get in the habit of creating your own day. Even if you only ever advance that far, you will be way ahead of most. However, you can and should go deeper as you get more comfortable with having a daily schedule.

I'd like to share an example of a more comprehensive daily schedule—and the one I happen to have on hand is my own! Review it, and then I will give you some thoughts on how to use it to create your own personal schedule.

PERSONAL DAILY SCHEDULE

5:00 a.m.: Wake up, take our dog out, get coffee or smoothie ready, and quickly check emails for any emergency or priority ones and glance at my calendar.

5:15–6:15 a.m.: Coffee with my wife, Sally, while listening to music or just quiet, complete daily journals, and cell phone ringer off. Journaling includes a top ten grateful list, intention statements or daily affirmations, and top three priority action items to have a successful day.

6:15–6:30 a.m.: Brush teeth, go to the bathroom if coffee worked (LOL), and get ready to work out and take morning vitamins.

Hypervibe Vibration machine for five minutes while looking in the mirror and saying affirmations.

6:30–7:30 a.m.: Begin workout, usually forty-five to sixty minutes (see Chapter 2 for options).

7:30–7:45 a.m.: Infrared heat sauna for ten to fifteen minutes; I shave in the sauna very easily when sweating, listen to meditation music or do breathing exercises or just relax.

7:45–8:00 a.m.: Shower (cold water for the first minute), get dressed and ready for the day.

8:00 a.m.–12:00 p.m.: Top three work priority items, scheduled calls or Zooms, and client meetings.

12:00–1:00 p.m.: Lunch break, get outside for ten to fifteen minutes, shut cell ringer off.

1:00–3:30 p.m.: Continue on the top three priority items, scheduled call or Zooms, and client meetings, plus any urgent matters that come up during the day.

3:30–4:00 p.m.: Healthy snack or afternoon coffee/smoothie, discuss with my wife and daughter what we have going on that day and see if we can help each other if we have spare time.

4:00–5:00 p.m.: Finish up priority items, clean up emails, desktop, desk area, and review calendar for next day.

5:00–6:00 p.m.: Watch a Mindvalley program and/or go for a walk or play with our dog.

6:00–7:00 p.m.: Dinner, play with Sophie, shut the cell phone ringer off, and do not discuss business unless necessary. When done eating, we will use that time to catch up with friends and family. Notice we waited until after we ate and relaxed with our ringers off.

7:00–8:00 p.m.: Wellness time, PEMF, red-light therapy, and whole-body vibration, or just quality alone time with Sally.

8:00–9:30 p.m.: Watch TV; we focus on recorded shows to avoid commercials; we stopped watching news and live a much happier life for it, and avoid harsh reality TV. (Our favorite is *Beat Bobby Flay* or *Guy's Grocery Games*.)

9:30–10:00 p.m.: Get ready for bed, get the house set for the morning, and read a few pages each night from a book of our choice; avoid TV thirty minutes before going to bed.

10:00 p.m.: Bedtime; we share things that were positive that happened during the day and usually play a twenty- to thirty-minute meditation to fall asleep to.

EVERY SLOT IS PLANNED OUT

One thing you will see right away is I plan out every time slot. Detailed planning like this might look too suffocating—until you try it. **It is true freedom, because you are the master of your day, not its victim.**

Some people fear this will mean living out each day like a robot. That is never how I feel. For one, I take days off for vacations and other breaks. And when life happens, I let it happen and simply address what needs to be addressed. All that aside, it is not robotic to plan things *I want* to accomplish. It is the opposite of robotic, because it is me as a unique individual deciding for myself how to plan out my own days.

FORGET THE MILE-HIGH CLUB; JOIN THE 5:00 A.M. CLUB

GETTING UP EARLY SETS THE TONE FOR THE DAY

If you study top performers, most of them are early risers. In fact, you may very well have heard references to the **5:00 a.m. Club.** It's not a real organization but a way to point out that super-successful people tend to get up around this time.

Early rising sets you up for a day where you feel empowered and in control. It's peaceful. There's no sounds of neighborhood construction, no loud lawnmowers, and no garbage being picked up. It is a magical time, so join me in being a member of the 5:00 a.m. Club.

Everything feels clearer and calmer in this environment. You'll note that very early on in my schedule, I have time to journal and to organize the priorities for my day.

I also exercise early. My recommendation is for a workout that creates some sweat because that gets your physical energy primed for the day. However, some mornings that may not be possible, so you'll do something less strenuous. Also, refer to Daily Wellness Ideas in Chapter 2 for recommendations on how you can best use this time.

TIME FOR HEALTH, TIME FOR LEARNING, TIME FOR RELATIONSHIPS

It's a common mistake to think of your daily schedule as simply a work-related schedule. "I have this meeting at this time, and then I have lunch with a client, and then I have to respond to emails, etc."

In an ideal daily schedule, you will make sure you are building time in to create abundance in *all areas* of your life. Besides health, you'll want to structure in time for learning and inspiration. For example, note that between 5:00 and 6:00 p.m., I have created a slot to watch a Mindvalley program or other learning sources.

It is also important to carve out time every day for your relationships. Some people are surprised by this advice. Don't you end up seeing your spouse and kids regularly being under the same roof?

What matters is the quality of the time you are spending with the most important people in your life. Most of us get so busy that when we are together, it can be challenging to enjoy it. It always seems to be about getting somebody somewhere or some mundane household matter. Some of that will be unavoidable, but the way to offset it is to plan time during each day to be present with each other.

Maybe a walk or a meditation. Agreeing on a show everyone can enjoy. Whatever it is, plan it. Then do it. And watch your relationships get stronger.

One tip I will give those readers who are a parent of multiple children: **When possible, build one-on-one time with each child.** As our daughters grew up, I would make a point of scheduling a breakfast or lunch alone with each of them on occasion. This does so much to send the message that you value time spent with them as unique individuals. It's also just plain enjoyable!

OTHER STUFF THAT'S GOOD TO KNOW

- **Turn the Ringer/Notifications Off:** Who is in charge, your phone or you? Have set times during the day where you shut off all ringers and notifications. Early morning quiet time, at lunch, and family time are some of the best times to do that. And, of course, overnight do not have your phone on and have it away from your bed. (If it is a must to leave it on, place it at least six feet from your bed.)

- **Declutter Your Workspace:** At the end of each workday, I make sure my desk is clear. That way, my mind starts the next workday clear, fresh, and ready to tackle that day's priorities first thing.

- **Create Weekly and Monthly Events, Too:** The example I shared above is one of my normal daily schedules, but there is of course variety from day to day. You may have things like a weekly date night, a monthly get-together with a social group, or a biweekly staff meeting at work. Your personal daily schedule can always accommodate. In fact, it will allow you to be more present during whatever you are doing because you have already allotted the time for it.

IT'S NOT ABOUT CONTROL; IT'S ABOUT CHOICES

I admit I am blessed to be able to work from a home office and that helps me stay in control of my schedule. Although I do travel a fair amount for business, it is still nice not having a daily commute or having a big group office where anyone can knock on my door at any moment.

Also, our beautiful daughters are grown, and so time running around, attending school events, and so forth is no longer a factor. I'm sure many of you reading this have those kinds of obligations in your life right now.

You may be thinking that you cannot create your day down to the level of detail that I am advocating in this chapter. And even if you could, you're sure it would have a lot more distractions and mundane duties than mine does. I have three answers to that for you to consider:

- You may be right that the specifics of your schedule will be different and you may currently have more additional duties outside of work than I do. It does not matter—a planned-out daily schedule can be just as effective for you as for me. You will still be creating your day; you'll simply be accounting for those other obligations. **Just make sure you are intentional with the time you do have,** and you will discover more abundance in your life.

- You can always fall back on the 3 Anchors discussed earlier in this chapter. If you are overwhelmed at the moment at the thought of creating a fully detailed personal daily schedule, then rely on using those three key anchors and build up to a more detailed plan later.

- There is also the possibility that you are looking for reasons for this not to work! Do not feel bad about that; it is something we all sometimes do when faced with trying to make an important positive change. But fight through it and make the change; you will be glad you did. **Remember, you always have time for what is most important in your life!**

Let me give you an example of what change can look like.

. . .

Let's say you're a successful small business owner. You have anywhere from five to one hundred-plus employees, most of them reporting to a physical office every day. Although you are pleased with your financial success, you often feel like your day runs you and not the other way around. It can make you feel ragged and question why you work so hard only to feel this way.

There is a solution, and it is to get control of your days by creating them instead of reacting to them. Here are three concrete steps you can take to have more abundance in your life.

Train your gatekeeper. With a company this size, you may have an assistant. It is important that you train that assistant to know that their number one job is as a gatekeeper for access to you. The assistant needs to know what time is blocked off as "disturb me only with a truly urgent issue."

Once you have a regular daily schedule that both your assistant and key staff know, you will be surprised how much more focused and productive your day is. Everyone now knows that from 9:30 a.m. to 11:00 a.m. you are devoted to working on your top three priorities that day and that you should only be disturbed for a very good reason.

Create a culture of problem solvers. Most successful business owners are smart and savvy, and so the staff regularly come to you with questions and problems to solve. If you are like many business leaders, your first inclination is to use your smarts to come up with an answer or take on the problem yourself.

Try this instead: Retrain your response when anyone on your staff brings a question or problem to your attention. Say something like, "What's one or two solutions you thought of before you came into my office?" If the employee does not have an answer, request that they go and think about it.

You might be surprised to discover that most of the time, the employee figures out how to resolve it themselves. This gives you much more time to spend on the big picture of your business and your top priorities. You can even get home earlier for dinner and spend more time on your relationships.

REFLECTION TIME

I would also recommend whether a business owner or a person building a career takes a few minutes at the end of each day to reflect. Take this time to clean your desk or work area, and look at your schedule for the next day. Most importantly, ask yourself if there was anything you could have done better during the day that would help you improve for the following day.

HIGHLY SUCCESSFUL PEOPLE *CREATE* THEIR OWN DAYS

Let me sum up this chapter for you in three bullets:

- The most abundant people create their own days, and they do not spend them in reactive mode putting out fires. They carefully and intentionally think through the day's top priorities and then get them completed first.

- People who create their own days are tenacious about it and at a minimum always use the 3 anchors to have a good and productive day.

- You will always struggle to maintain consistent abundance in all areas of your life unless you learn to master your own daily schedule. Remember, you are the boss of your life!

CHAPTER 6

TENACIOUS THOUGHT LEADERS

LEARN FROM THE BEST OF THE BEST

Truly successful people find other more successful people to role-model and imitate.

Abundance is everywhere, including the internet.

Of course, internet abundance is a double-edged sword. On the downside, there is just so much out there that it can be hard to find the nuggets of pure gold among all the mediocre or even bad advice posted every day. **The internet also can be a distraction machine.** Without some discipline, we end up going down rabbit holes, wasting our brain space on things that either do not matter or we can't control.

But the positive side of the internet abundance delivers fantastic value. Think how incredible it is that there is top-quality information, inspiration, and guidance available with just a few keystrokes. And so much of it is *free*.

This is another opportunity for gratitude, to remind ourselves of our good fortune to live in a time and place that allows these opportunities. But of course, an opportunity means nothing until you take advantage of it.

What I'm going to provide you in this chapter is an extremely efficient way to view some of the best quality content available on the internet without having to search and find it yourself. Or if you already have found some but want more, here is a shortcut to finding it fast.

MY FAVORITE THOUGHT LEADERS IN THE WORLD ON YOUTUBE

I have watched a lot of videos on YouTube, and what follows is my curated list of content that delivers value that is off the charts. For each video, I give you a very brief synopsis of why it is worth your time and provide the runtime so you'll know how much time to set aside to watch any particular video.

None of the videos are longer than twenty minutes and many are much shorter. That's intentional. It allows you to fit viewing around a busy schedule and also allows you to give them your full attention. These videos are free of fluff and you'll get so much out of them in a short period of time.

ONE AT A TIME OR GO FOR IT ALL?

There are two ways to use the recommendations below. Neither is right or wrong; it all depends on what will provide *you* with the most value.

One way is to consider this a complete tenacious abundance video course. To use this method, watch each video (the specific order does not matter). I do not recommend you watch them one on top of the other. These are so good that it can be tempting to do that, but that is not how to get the most value out of your viewing.

Instead, set aside a time each week to view a single video and then do a short reflection (either in a journal or just think about it). Note what you learned and how it could be useful and applicable in your own life.

If you do this, you will get a lot more value out of it than if you rush through them. Once you have completed the "course" (all the videos over a period of several weeks), you will be astounded by how much value you received for free from some of the top minds in the world.

The other option is to choose the videos that seem most relevant to your specific needs at this point in your life. I have grouped the videos by category. For example, if you are a business owner who wants to level up your skills as a leader, watch the videos under the "Leadership" heading.

Or if you recently had a failure or setback and you are feeling a little bruised, go to the "Self-Esteem" category and get perspective and build yourself back up.

I encourage you to do a short reflection after viewing and give yourself at least one actionable item to implement from what you learned.

Note: URLs for all the videos are provided below, but you

can also get access to all these links in one place by visiting www.tenaciousabundance.com.

SELF-ESTEEM

Sean Stephenson

https://www.youtube.com/watch?v=VaRO5-V1uK0

Runtime 10:26

Sean was one of the most respected members of the Genius Network and was always a shining light. He also had a remarkable sense of humor. If he made his life truly incredible and felt great about himself, then anyone can. Watching this always reminds me to never be a victim and to shake off self-pity when something doesn't go the way I wanted.

Marisa Peer

https://www.youtube.com/watch?v=HzMXtu93iQI

Runtime 9:41

Marisa Peer is the British equivalent of Tony Robbins and certainly no beginner in living an abundant life. She has been teaching for nearly four decades, is exceptionally well-spoken, and gives clear and easy-to-understand solutions for self-esteem. Marisa is a huge proponent of having her clients write "I Am Enough" on their mirrors and on cell phone screens and to recite it daily. As I said in Chapter 1, I'm a big believer in this affirmation as well and have felt the results in my own life. I believe if more people thought they were enough, it would solve 90+ percent of their problems.

→ marisapeer.com

Joel Osteen

https://www.youtube.com/watch?v=MTxQP1KYqoU

Runtime 4:13

Joel Osteen talks about the power of "I am" and how important it is for us to make sure whatever follows I am is self-empowering and not negative. He explains the importance of positive self-talk, especially when using the words "I am." This video is very short, but it is a powerful reminder of how to build ourselves up and not tear ourselves down.

→ joelosteen.com

LEADERSHIP

Coach Lou Holtz

https://www.youtube.com/watch?v=0wMmcoPTmAs

Runtime 6:27

Coach Holtz gives some priceless advice on leadership and life. If you have not encountered Coach Holtz previously, you are in for a treat. His delivery is fun and captivating as he weaves in his personal story. Coach Holtz provides a window into his life growing up and the adversity he faced. Then he follows it up with solid advice that resonates with the story: Be proactive in helping others and always do what is right, even if it is not popular. Watching this is to see what true leadership looks like.

Coach John Wooden

https://www.youtube.com/watch?v=SF-G3fcFJgw

Runtime 3:58

I feel very blessed to have met Coach Wooden personally at his home in California and to have had the opportunity to spend the day with him. He is the definition of leadership and a life teacher. After spending time with this extremely genuine and generous man, I can tell you he lived what he preached. He was a shining example of what he tells others in this video: to be a living steward of humanity. It is my truest honor to have called him a friend.

→ coachwooden.com

Bo Eason

https://vimeo.com/boeason/review/85790757/e4611efbbf

Runtime 16:10

Bo has a unique style of captivating the listener and delivering the message in a way that you will not forget it. It's impossible to not realize you are encountering a truly amazing human being as you watch this. This is like the best kind of history lesson: he covers the three traits of leaders for the past 2,000 years. One of the best videos on leadership ever. Generosity is one of the traits, but you will be surprised by what he means by that and how well he explains it using NFL Hall of Famer Jerry Rice as the example. Bo Eason is at a whole other level of energy and motivation than most speakers on the planet.

→ boeason.com

Admiral William McRaven

https://youtu.be/pxBQLFLei70

Runtime 19:26

Admiral McRaven is the real deal. To become a Navy SEAL is ridiculously tough, and his delivery and content in this video reflects that. It lays out very plainly the steps necessary to become a true leader. There is no room for fluff when training for the Navy SEALs, and there is no fluff in this video either.

MOTIVATIONAL

Tony Robbins

www.youtube.com/watch?v=CVP1CwEBz_Y&t=4s

Runtime 15:13

Clearly the king of motivation and in my eyes the most effective human being on the planet for helping others change. In this amazing video, he will discuss the eight things that truly matter! This video changed my life and refocused me on what is most important.

→ tonyrobbins.com

Tucker Max

https://www.youtube.com/watch?v=EJVh_PU4Qdw

Runtime 13:33

Founder of Scribe Media, Tucker is just a straightforward person who tells you like it is and his story and advice are spot-on—and his humor is great. Everyone has something important to share, and Tucker has created a system for helping others do just that.

Evan Carmichael

https://www.youtube.com/c/Evancarmichael

Watch anything on his YouTube channel!

Evan is simply a wonderful person who wakes up every day truly passionate to help others. He has interviewed some of the top performers in the world and always gets their top ten strategies/tips for success. It is so motivating to hear what to focus on from the most successful people on the planet.

Ed Mylett

https://www.edmylett.com/podcasts/

Any of his podcasts!

Since this is a podcast, you have the option to just listen, but you can find videos of the interviews on the website listed above. Ed has become a podcast star because of his great interviewing skills, and it has attracted some of the most sought-after high performers on the planet. (This is the podcast that I heard Howard Behar on, the story I told in Chapter 1.)

Regularly watching or listening to Ed is a much better use of your time than watching trivial TV shows or negative news or New Jersey housewives.

NEXT-LEVEL THINKING

Mike Rowe

https://www.youtube.com/watch?v=ebn9KSTi_yU

Runtime 9:20

Mike Rowe, in his witty and well-spoken manner, shares his thoughts on the next generation and gives an extraordinarily candid interview about life and work. I love this man's humor and his ability to "truth tell"—he adds so much value. This video will give you a clear understanding of how blue-collar work has been devalued and how to get back to basics.

→ mikerowe.com

James Clear
https://www.youtube.com/watch?v=jeqaIYchAI0
Runtime 10:00

James Clear is the modern-day master of habits, and trust me that habits maketh the man! He is so insightful and he crafts his thoughts carefully. I also recommend signing up for his superb 3-2-1 newsletter that he sends out every Thursday. The pearls of wisdom he sends out are terrific, and he always ends with a question to ask yourself that never fails to make you think.

→ jamesclear.com

BIOHACKING

Dave Asprey
www.youtube.com/watch?v=fqseGkj77ic
Runtime 9:32

Dave Asprey is known as the founder of Bulletproof Coffee, but he is also the creator of biohacking. He always tests what he teaches on himself first before sharing it with others. Dave also hosts a Biohacking Conference every year because he is truly committed to sharing cutting-edge ideas. This man is just plain amazing and he loves to share!

→ daveasprey.com

MONEY

Ken Honda

https://www.youtube.com/watch?v=3PZ1oaKh2eI

Runtime 19:53

Japan's best-known secret, Ken has written over fifty books on money. He is the real deal and was wealthy before he started writing. He was mentored by the Warren Buffet of Japan, Master Wahei. Ken makes some amazing points about money that will help you better understand it. When someone has gotten results like Ken Honda, enabling retirement at a young age, listen to them. Also, if you listen and take action, you will watch your relationship with money improve.

→ kenhonda.com

LAW OF ATTRACTION

Bob Proctor

https://www.youtube.com/watch?v=zJ7tJApsKCo

Runtime 10:12

Bob Proctor is known as the grandfather of motivational speaking, and that moniker is well-earned. He is without doubt one of the all-time greatest motivators and has always had the sincere intention of helping others and sharing his knowledge. There has always been something special about Bob Proctor and he understands vibrations in the Universe like very few do. Give this a view to see what I mean.

→ proctorgallagherinstitute.com

Dr. Wayne Dyer

https://www.youtube.com/watch?v=BWEy8brAuRA

Runtime 10:05

This is Dr. Dyer's last video message, and he clearly saved the best for last. Please watch this and share with others because his advice is priceless. You can also see how clearly gifted of a person he was. We can easily reprogram ourselves if we understand how simple it is to accomplish, and Dr. Dyer makes that completely understandable.

→ drwaynedyer.com

That is the best of the best, and it is all free. Quite honestly, it would be foolish not to spend time with these top performers who share their top beliefs and proven strategies.

CHAPTER 7

MUSIC: THE HEALTHY WONDER DRUG

Try to imagine the movie *Jaws* without those two famous notes played over and over. You know exactly what I am talking about because anyone who has ever seen that movie can hear those scary notes to this day. I guarantee if you blasted it over speakers at the beach, everyone is immediately sprinting out of the water and onto dry land.

Or how about *Rocky*? If the booming sound of "Gonna Fly Now" starts playing, I bet you cannot help but feel a rush of inspiration and think of Rocky training like a madman. You hear that song and your mood gets an instant hit of adrenaline.

Or as I mentioned in an earlier chapter, my wife cries during the last scene in *Planes, Trains, and Automobiles*, and that has a lot to do with the song "Everytime You Go" playing in the background.

What is going on here? How is it that millions of us can instantly be put in touch with fundamental emotions based on a song?

Because that's what music does. It anchors movies, ties them in our brain to certain emotions and mindsets. And that is also what music can do for us in general.

This is the shortest chapter in the book, but do not let that mislead you about its importance. Music is one of the most powerful tools in our toolkit when we consciously use it. To put it another way:

Music is one of the most undervalued resources for motivating us, for making us happy, and for serving as anchors for moods and moments of our lives. I call music the original mood-altering, non fattening wonder drug, and I am not exaggerating.

What I want to do in this chapter is convince you that music is a powerful aid in bringing more abundance in our lives, and if we use it tenaciously and intentionally, we will get more value out of it.

THE TRUE POWER OF ANCHORING WITH MUSIC

I think we should all create a playlist for our own lives. (I share mine below.) And we should break it up into major categories.

We should have an overall life theme song. Mine is "Jump" by Van Halen. That's because "nothing gets me down," and when in doubt, I figure "you might as well JUMP!" It reminds me of who I am and what I believe, and it does it in a way that drives my energy through the roof.

Here are other categories you should consider having songs for:

- Relationships

- Soulmate

- Motivational

- Inspiration

- Workout

- Gratitude

- Reflection

- Other categories important to you, where you want to anchor moments to the right feelings

The idea is to create a number of songs under each category that you can use as anchors to get motivated or get more enjoyment out of moments.

For example, workout songs. I have a two-minute exercise drill I love to use as a break in my day. For this, I use the Dazy Chain song "Level Up," which happens to be both exactly two minutes and contains the kind of pump-up beat that keeps me fired up during the mini workout.

I also use "Sexy and I Know It" and "Head and Heart" as cardio workout songs due to their great beats. Exercise is so much more fun when you do it to music. When you are trying to establish and maintain a habit, why would you not use something that makes you want to do it more?

This goes beyond exercise, though. If I have a big meeting coming up and I know I need an extra edge to be at my absolute best, there is nothing like blasting some Bill Conti "Going the Distance" from the *Rocky* soundtrack to get me primed.

Music can also be a fantastic way to access great memories. To this day, I remember driving down the road about a quarter century ago while MC Hammer cranked out "Too Legit to Quit" over my car stereo. I was headed toward what at the time was a big meeting for me with the General Nutrition Center (GNC) franchise owner about a product I had created called the Belt Buddy that I wanted him to carry in his stores. Anytime I hear that song, that happy memory comes flooding back.

Music is also a great way to remind yourself of the people you care about the most. Whenever my phone rings and the ringtone is the "Most Beautiful Girl in the World," I know it is one of my daughters or my granddaughter calling.

My wife and I love the song "Bless the Open Road" because it reminds us that we were and are meant to be together. Wouldn't it be good to have a song that can help you hit the reset button after a disagreement or to just remind you how much that person means to you?

BRAIN ENTRAINMENT USING BINAURAL BEATS

There's another kind of sound you can use to improve the abundance in your life besides songs, and that is binaural beat technology. That first word sounds like a mouthful, but the idea behind this is very simple.

A binaural beat is an illusion created by the brain when you listen to two tones with slightly different frequencies at the same time. Your brain interprets the two tones as a beat of its own. The two tones align with your brain waves to produce a beat with a different frequency.

As an example, if you play a frequency like 12 Hertz in one ear and 10 Hertz in the other ear, it creates a certain kind of brain wave reaction using both your right and left brain. So different frequencies set you up for different things. Success, relaxation, weight loss, money, focus, sleep, creativity, and so on.

Binaural beats are something new under the sun, a true hack for the brain. Aristotle said, "Give me a child until he is seven and I will show you the man." Back in ancient times, this was probably true—whatever had been programmed into your brain by age seven was hard to overwrite. But this great technology opens up a new way. It gives you a chance to choose what programs you would like your brain to run and not the other way around.

Binaural beats can get you synced for profound levels of calm, focus, or creativity. It will also help you meditate and sleep more deeply. The best website I have found to both explain this and to provide binaural beats for different needs is called Brain Sync and it is run by Kelly Howell.

MY PERSONAL SONG LIST OR CREATE YOUR OWN

Below is my personal list of songs. You may find some that you want to steal for your own playlist. That's my purpose in sharing it, so please do!

Others of you will want to use it as an example only and customize it with songs that will put you in the best mindset for any particular situation.

Truly grasp what a great resource music is for fueling more abundance in your life.

Purpose	Artist	Song
My Life Theme Song	Van Halen	"Jump"
Relationship	Blessid Union	"Hey, Leonardo"
Relationship	Edwin McCain	"I Could Not Ask for More"
Relationship	Florida Georgia Line	"Second Guessing"
Relationships	Kristian Bush	"Forever Now"
Soulmate	Rascal Flatts	"Bless the Broken Road"
Soulmate	Tina Turner	"Simply the Best"
Wife & Daughters	Prince	"Most Beautiful Girl in the World"
Fathers & Sons	The Chainsmokers	"Something Just like This"
Motivation	Bill Conti	"Going the Distance"
Motivation	AC/DC	"Thunderstruck"
Motivation	Journey	"Don't Stop Believing"
Motivation	Red Ryder	"Lunatic Fringe"
Awesome Day	Van Halen	"Top of the World"

Inspirational	Rascal Flatts	"My Wish"
Inspirational	Pete Townsend	"Let My Love Open the Door"
Inspirational	Belinda Carlisle	"Heaven Is a Place on Earth"
Inspirational	Pink	"A Million Dreams"
Inspirational	New Radicals	"You Get What You Give"
Workout	LMFAO	"Sexy and I Know It"
Workout	Dazy Chain	"Level Up"
Workout	Joel Corry	"Head and Heart"
Change	Haddayway	"Life"
Gratitude	Thomas Newman	"Walkaway"
Gratitude	Tim McGraw	"Humble and Kind"
Gratitude	Mercy Me	"I Can Only Imagine"
Coming Home	Motley Crew	"Home, Sweet Home"
Reflection	Christopher Cross	"Sailing"
Reflection	James Horner/London Symphony	"Braveheart"
Reflection	Thomas Wander & Harald Kloser	"Midway Main Theme"
Reflection	Alan Silvestri	"Suite from Forrest Gump"

CHAPTER 8

I AM BLESSED

Feeling truly blessed is where tenacious abundance all comes together.

Knowing deep down that you are blessed supports all the other areas of abundance. It also gives you a feeling of emotional well-being and gratitude for everything you are and have.

Sounds great, right? But maybe a little vague, too. You just can't snap your fingers and be blessed. How do you "bring it all together"? Does it mean we work harder at happiness, health, wealth, and wisdom and then just hope everything falls into place and we start feeling blessed?

No, there's more to it than adding up all the other areas of abundance and saying, "I am now officially blessed!" You can intentionally cultivate a blessed mindset with specific thoughts and actions.

First, you need to grasp the two fundamental keys to feeling blessed:

1. Understand how unique you are (and how unique everyone else is, too).

2. Work intentionally at feeling more gratitude about your life and all the good people and things in it.

I am going to give you some specific reflections and actions to bring a better understanding of these concepts. Following this advice will create an amazing sense of peace and abundance in your life.

THE UNIQUENESS OF *YOU*

When an original painting by a famous artist goes up for sale, it goes for millions and millions of dollars. Why? Because the collector knows there is only one original and that means it will hold its value—or more likely, climb in value.

Or think about a special moment in the life of one of our loved ones, let's say a high school graduation. We celebrate and cherish that. Not only because it is an accomplishment but also because it is a unique event in that person's life. It will not be happening for them again.

If we place such a high value on unique possessions and unique events, how much more should we value each unique individual? How much more should you value yourself?

You are completely irreplaceable. There is no one with exactly the same eyes, fingerprints, teeth, tone of voice, laugh, skin color, personality—the list could go on forever. Reflect on that and value it.

This insight could also help with some of our divisions. It seems like political, religious, racial, and other kinds of strife keep growing lately. We are not going to settle all this anytime soon, but I believe a start would be an acknowledgment by all of the uniqueness of every single person, and that means valuing every single person. On the flip side, our commonality is that we are all part of this unique, incredible human race.

It reminds me of a small but telling example during the COVID-19 pandemic. You may remember early on, there was a lot of talk about who was an essential worker and who was not essential. I understand there was a perceived need to sort this out, but those labels are extremely unhelpful. **Everyone is essential.** We all matter, and whatever contribution we make is essential.

STOP WISHING YOU WERE TALLER OR SMARTER OR SKINNIER OR...

If you have read this book from the beginning, you will remember that one of the first points in the book is that you need to understand that *you are enough*. And that goes right along with understanding how unique you are.

Too many times, we torture ourselves. We wish we were taller. Or had ripped abs. Or we were more beautiful or weren't going bald. As you know, I am all for working on changing what can be changed. But accept the rest and remember that *you are enough, you have enough, and you do enough*.

APPRECIATE BEING A HUMAN BECAUSE IT'S SPECIAL

One thing I can confidently say is that no gorillas, dolphins, or pigs will be reading this book. That might sound a little trite at first, but do we ever stop and fully appreciate what we can do as human beings? We can anticipate things. We can communicate in complex ways. We can read books like this and try to get a little better in how we live our lives.

Yet we always seem to look for reasons to be down on the human race, when what we should be doing is treasuring all our gifts. **Remember to include yourself in this treasuring, because the person staring back at you in the mirror will be with you forever.** Always respect yourself and your abilities.

MORE GRATITUDE, BETTER ATTITUDE

The other key to feeling blessed is to train your emotions and your thoughts until you become a person who is filled with gratitude. We all know people who have a knack for taking everything in their life and bending it toward the negative.

Sometimes we tend to think this is all just personality and we cannot do anything to change it. But there are specific ways to increase gratitude, and you can make a decision to be a grateful person. **It's impossible to be negative and unhappy when you are feeling grateful. So choose gratitude—period.**

Ever Widening Circles of Gratitude

Here is one of my favorite exercises for keeping gratitude front and center in our lives and to remind us of our deep connection to other human beings on this planet. I learned this from Dr. Scott Mills when he appeared on a Ken Honda Mindvalley program.

This can be done as a form of meditation, or you can just do it informally by simply giving it some thought. Here is how to do it.

Be still in your mind and imagine yourself at the center of a small circle. Surrounding you are your family, those who love you and care for you the most. Think of how they support you and how grateful you are for that.

Next, widen the circle to include friends who make your life more enjoyable and memorable. The ones who call and ask how you are doing when you have hit a rough patch. Think also of your employees or coworkers, who help you make a living, and hopefully make your workday enjoyable. Pause and consider how intertwined our lives are and how grateful we should be for friends and those we work with.

Now widen the circle even further and think of the ordinary actions of others that support all of us and make our lives livable. The people who collect your trash from the curb. The clerk at the grocery store. The workers repairing the roads we all drive on. The people who installed the electrical grid that powers your home. You get the idea. Think of as many as you can. It's truly stunning the network of human interactions and how much it supports what we take for granted every day. Only this time, do not take it for granted; think how appreciative you are to have all this in your life.

Widen it again. For example, it is not just the grocery cashier or stocker we should think about. What about the delivery drivers who brought all the food and other goods? The farmers who grew the food and raised the livestock. The distribution center workers who filled the store's order. This could go on almost infinitely, and that is just the grocery store. You could do the same thing for trash pickup (who built the trucks, who works at the landfill, etc.) and any number of other goods and services.

This is the key insight: the *incredible number of people* behind all these everyday interactions and transactions who support us and make our lives better. **We need to realize how many people we don't even know touch our lives in a positive way.**

Notice that this exercise works because it encourages us to think very specifically about how we are supported in our daily lives by others. Instead of a general "we should be grateful for others," this one truly makes us think and immediately increases our gratitude.

This beautiful exercise also has long-term effects. It will come to mind in situations when you are being served by others. You will find yourself feeling more patient toward those serving you and treat them with even greater respect. That is the power of gratitude, and it brings blessings to both you and others.

I strongly recommend doing this exercise on a regular basis. Your sense of connection and well-being will go way up.

Gratitude at the Beginning and End of Every Day

Here is one of the best habits you can get into at the beginning and end of every day. Keep a gratitude journal and set aside a few minutes first thing in the morning and a few minutes before bedtime to jot down what you are grateful for.

Be creative and expansive when thinking of what you are grateful for. Things like your heart beating without you telling it to, or fresh air to breathe, or even simply a paper clip that holds your papers together. The list is endless.

Some days, you can write down big things. Something that went right with your business or career. How happy you are with a family relationship that is going well. That a friend overcame a serious illness.

But do not focus only on big things. For one, big things do not always go our way, and if we rely on that, our gratitude will be dependent on circumstances that are sometimes beyond our control.

Train yourself to remember all the amazing things we take for granted that 99 percent of people who ever lived did not have access to, and many still don't.

Things that we can and should feel gratitude for:

- That huge variety of food available to us all the time.

- That we have the freedom to travel when and where we want to so easily.

- That we can marry whom we want to (that is not true in every time and place).

- We can brush our teeth every day and have access to quality dental care (something the overwhelming

majority of people in history did not, and many
still don't).

- We have indoor plumbing, which makes getting water,
keeping ourselves clean, and getting rid of human
waste easy.

- We have heating and cooling systems to keep
us comfortable.

- Access to amazing healthcare.

- This list could easily go on for pages…and I hope it
does in your own gratitude journal!

Doing this every morning and every night sets the exact right
tone for the start and close of your day and promotes a spirit of
abundance in your life.

STOP COMPARING UP OR DOWN

When we analyze our own lives, we tend to compare ourselves
to those with more than us. We worry about what others have
that we do not. Is our house good enough? What kind of car
are we driving compared to the shiny new one in our neighbor's
driveway?

Or maybe we are envious of someone else's promotion or
honor or recognition, and we feel worse about ourselves in com-
parison. **Comparing up works against gratitude and feeling
abundantly blessed.**

Do we think to compare the other way? That 3 billion people on this planet are living on $2 or less a day? That there

are so many people who spend their days just getting enough to subsist?

And here's the thing. Many of these people are not miserable. I'm sure it can be a hard life, but most are still able to laugh, cry, feel joy, fall in love, get married, have kids, and enjoy the natural beauty of the world.

What was it you wanted to complain to me about again?

In all seriousness, we need to check ourselves and be humble and grateful for all the goods and services and conveniences and housing that we take completely in stride, never acknowledging how incredibly fortunate it is.

BE GRATEFUL FOR YOUR CHALLENGES

Do you know some of the most miserable, screwed-up people on the planet? Kids who grew up with wealthy parents who handed them everything and who were protected from every problem and challenge. I am not trying to pick on them here; I actually feel sorry that this happened to them.

Why exactly is it a problem that they were so shielded? Shouldn't it logically follow that a rich and protected life is one of nonstop fun, ease, and leisure? What happens is that these kids may never grow as much as they could, because they have not been tested and challenged. **We become mature and able to live as fully independent human beings when we are forced to figure out solutions to our own problems.**

Think about this the next time you are weighed down with troubles or are struggling to solve a problem. Instead of bemoaning it or giving up on it, be grateful for it. Express gratitude for this chance to take a step forward, rise to the occasion, and do your best to solve it or accept it. **Remember, life happens for us, not to us. Attitude is paramount.**

So when you are down, remember that problems transform into growth when you learn to solve them instead of thinking of them as insurmountable obstacles. What seems at first as a block to blessedness may turn out to be a door to welcome more abundance in your life. As the Rascal Flatts song "My Wish" states, if you find the door closed, keep on walking until you find a window. **Be grateful for your challenges and setbacks.**

HEAVEN IS TRULY A PLACE ON EARTH

Belinda Carlisle has a song with a similar title, and I love that mindset. Okay, admittedly sometimes earth can feel less than heavenly. But the more we think of it as a positive place to be, the better things and relationships we attract into our lives.

None of us can know for sure what happens when we pass away, and the idea of heaven is something most people think of only in terms of a possible afterlife. But I like to think that heaven is about right here, right now. It's in the magic of our own choices, the ones we make about how we live our lives every day.

There have been many times in my life where I went through something that at the time I thought, "What the heck is going on?" or "Why me?" But then later, I found out that what happened in my past helped me in my future. I truly believe, through my own experience and observing others, that what we put out into the universe comes back to us. **Always focus on what you want to happen instead of what you don't want to happen.**

The story of losing my dad at age sixteen is a great example of this. At the time, I thought my world was ending and I felt so lost. I wondered how I could possibly move forward without my father.

Many years later, it led me to owning a health club, starting a financial/insurance company, and spending most of my adult life focusing on how to take care of myself and help others. Not a day has gone by since his death that I have not thought of my dad, and of course I have missed him. However, on that dreaded day in 1982 and during the hard times that followed, I would not have imagined that I could have also learned how to use that harsh experience as fuel to serve others and myself.

It's not just the most difficult experiences either. How we think of the "small stuff" of life will also make a big difference in how blessed we feel.

For example, I have an acquaintance who had a string of bad house malfunctions happen one on top of the other. Unpleasant, no doubt. But then he said to me, "If something bad is going to happen, it's going to happen to me."

I am sure it was said out of frustration, but this is exactly the kind of mindset and disaffirmation you want to avoid. It will lead to you dwelling on problems, and it will attract more of them. I cannot prove that like a science equation, but I can tell you that people who look for bad luck and problems tend to find them. On the other hand, people who expect life to be closer to heaven on earth find abundance. I've seen it over and over, too many times to be a coincidence.

Let me lay this out in concrete terms. A person who will attract negative things will think and talk in these patterns:

- I'm trapped in my job.

- I'm stuck in this relationship.

- I have the worst luck.

A person who will attract abundance thinks like this:

- Wow, I get to choose who I can marry and how many kids I want.

- I can go shopping and buy things that make my life better, anything from ice cream in whatever flavor I want to a car that can take me to all kinds of places.

- The economy is so big and there are so many things I am capable of doing that I can choose my job or what business I want to start. I don't need to take someone else's piece of the pie to be successful; there is enough pie for everyone.

I am sure you can spot the difference in mindset. Use your gratitude journal to talk to yourself in the abundance mindset and never tell yourself you are stuck.

LET THE UNIVERSE BRING YOU GOOD FORTUNE

I have witnessed business owners over the years beat themselves up because they feel like they need to beat last year by X percentage for it to be a good year. As you know, I am all for striving for higher achievement and incremental improvement.

But whether that desire for improvement is healthy or not depends on your motivation for wanting it and how far and fast you are trying to force it. Do not be tenacious about aiming for a certain result because you know your competitor got that result.

Do not be tenacious about wanting a bigger house because you think it will make you happier or to "keep up with the Joneses" as the saying has it.

Instead, be tenacious about the process, about doing the right things. Be tenacious in believing that the Universe will send you the right people at the right time to help you on your journey. Be tenacious about wanting to improve for your own sake, not because you feel less when you compare yourself to someone else.

Especially be tenacious about adding value to others, because what we give is what we get back. Think of it like how we breathe in and out to live. You can only breathe in so long before you are forced to breathe out and vice versa. In the same way, the more tenaciously you give value to others, the more you will get in return.

I would be remiss in not mentioning that I believe all of my success is tied to God blessing me. I have always felt as though I have had a guardian angel watching over me. **Whether you think it is God, the Universe, or some higher power, it is a key belief for a life of abundance.**

And always remember, you are enough. You have enough. You do enough. Keep going and be grateful for the journey.

THE POWER OF 3s
CHAPTER SUMMARY

Top Ways to Implement the Concepts in This Chapter

Three Habits/Hacks

1. Write down at least three to ten things you are grateful for each morning and then think of at least one to two great things that happened during the day before you go to sleep so it is last on your mind.

2. Realize there is always someone in the world worse off than you. Stop being a victim, think big picture, and choose to be grateful when challenged. Watch Joel Osteen Sunday morning for a positive and uplifting message to start your week.

3. Pray for others each night before going to bed; there's no better way to feel blessed than praying and thinking of others. When you focus on adding value and helping others, it is impossible to feel bad about yourself.

Three Key Beliefs

1. There is no one like me in the entire universe; I am a masterpiece of God.

2. Life does not happen to me; it happens for me.

3. A thought of gratitude gives me a much better attitude.

Three Key Questions

1. Who can I help today that is not able to repay me?

2. In what ways am I a blessing to others?

3. What in my life, family, friends, or career is a blessing to me today?

CONCLUSION

"Be yourself; everyone else is already taken."

—Oscar Wilde

For me, this conclusion is both easy and hard.

The hard part for me is choosing how to sum up everything in this book. I love the tenacious abundance in my own life and I have so much gratitude for all I have learned along my own journey from others that I would like to sum up everything in this book all over again.

But one of my guiding stars for this book has been to make it a practical and easy guide to implementing change a little at a time. And I know if you try to take in everything in this book all at once, you will struggle.

So I challenged myself to come up with the seven best ways to get more abundance in your life. I wanted this conclusion to be your launch point for being tenacious about it, and I know the simpler I make it, the more likely you are to go for it.

My hope is that you will see so much abundance from implementing these seven ways that you'll think, "Hey, maybe this Anthony guy is onto something!" Success will breed more success, and you can then return to this book again and again to add more of the habits, hacks, and strategies and keep getting more and more abundant.

Once I thought of it that way, then came the easy part. Because it is pure joy to share my absolute favorites with others. **Here is the best of the best, the top 7 ways to get more tenacious abundance in your own life:**

1. **Love yourself unconditionally and remember that you are unique.** Remember to be yourself as everyone else is taken. These thoughts have to be the foundation of everything good in your life. (Chapters 1 and 8 cover these topics.)

2. **Realize that you are enough.** Use the key affirmation of "I am enough. I have enough. I do enough" on a daily basis. (This is fully explained in Chapter 1.) Keep positive affirmations in front of you at all times! Successful people use great affirmations as their self-talk and you should as well.

3. **Great habits are life changing,** and you only need a few key ones to see massive impact. Always remember that new habits take far longer than the twenty-one days proclaimed often by the self-help industry. You need to do them at least ninety days to really wire them in, and in most cases even longer.

4. **The greatest wealth is your health.** Your health is so precious, and it gives you the energy to go after abundance in all other areas. Chapter 2 leaves you with no excuse for not becoming healthier, because it shows you easy ways to improve your physical health right away.

5. **Add value always and forever; it will serve you tenfold.** When you focus on adding value to others, you ultimately end up adding value to yourself. As my father stated, be a person who adds value and you will have a great life!

6. **Change will only happen if you get control of your personal daily schedule.** All the habits, hacks, and strategies in this book only work if you do them! You cannot implement anything consistently unless you learn to create your own day. Start off by using the three anchors fully explained in Chapter 5 (Personal Daily Schedule).

7. **Gratitude, Gratitude, GRATITUDE!** If you want to bring it all together and feel blessed and completely abundant, an attitude of gratitude is *the* keystone mindset. See Chapter 8 for practical ways to get more grateful for your life and its abundance.

Now stand up, take a deep breath, and smile big. Start your amazing journey toward living a life of tenacious abundance. In the spirit of Van Halen, jump!

.   .   .

Please feel free to reach out and let me know how this book changed your life, your company, or just a positive thought you have to share at info@tenaciousabundance.com or (407) 322-2555. You can also find links to many of the resources in this book on the website tenaciousabundance.com.

Live with tenacious abundance!
Anthony "Tenacious" Trupiano

FOR BUSINESS OWNERS

BRING TENACIOUS ABUNDANCE INTO YOUR COMPANY CULTURE

If you love the ideas in this book, imagine the power of giving a copy to the people who work for you. What would it be like to have a staff of abundantly happy, healthy, wealthy, and wise people serving each other and your customers? The results would be powerful. Here are some other creative and effective ideas for bringing this into your workplace.

A GRATITUDE BOARD IN THE BREAK ROOM

Have a place in the break room where people can post what or whom they are grateful for. It could be things in their personal life but also compliments about coworkers, what they like about their job, and so forth. Gratitude can be contagious.

ACCESS TO HEALTHY SNACKS

What is served at your meetings? Maybe stop the bagels, cream cheese, doughnuts, and so on and offer fresh fruits, veggies and dip, or similar. (By the way, I plead guilty to sometimes having brought unhealthy snacks for staff when I visit clients. I said I was abundant, not perfect!)

Also, make clean, healthy water easily available. A great idea would be getting your employees a company-branded twenty-six ounce Yeti with a straw for easy water consumption.

ENCOURAGE EXERCISE

Announce a walking club at work, where people get together for a brief brisk walk after lunch. Or perhaps have an empty office or gym space where people can go for a ten-minute isometric break or do the two-minute routine outlined in Chapter 2.

BATHROOM MIRROR AFFIRMATIONS

Use mirror markers for positive affirmations or messages to your employees. You can have some bedrock affirmations that serve as a reminder of the value your company adds to your customers. You can also have some affirmations that change from time to time to keep it fun. Always remember, you want messages that make people know they are valued.

TREATING YOUR EMPLOYEES WITH COMPASSION WHEN THEY NEED IT

It is important to remember that you send a message by how you respond to someone's time of trouble. If you are making a great deal of money, and one of your employees becomes ill, be understanding that this may cause them significant financial stress from taking time off from work. In these situations, giving them flexibility to resolve their issue is paramount. Try to walk in others' shoes before passing judgment. What is going on in our lives at 10:00 p.m. affects what we do at 10:00 a.m. in the office or at the jobsite and vice versa.

PROVIDE AMAZING BENEFITS

Since nearly 70 percent of all bankruptcies are caused by high medical expenses, it is important to find a cutting-edge solution to contain costs for your employees as well as your company. My friends Dr. David Berg and Dr. Janice Johnston have created a new affordable way to deliver quality healthcare that I believe is revolutionizing the industry. Their company is Redirect Health, and you can get additional information by visiting www.redirecthealth.com/tenacious or www.trupianoassociates.com.

HAVE AN AMAZING CPA FIRM ON YOUR TEAM

Creating a mastermind of professionals should start with an amazing CPA firm, and the best we have discovered over the past thirty-plus years of being self-employed is Ed Lloyd & Associates. They are a national CPA firm for businesses, and in my opinion, they are second to none with regard to expert guidance and superior service. Please feel free to contact them about your company at tenacious@elcpa.com.

BONUS IDEA: A PRESENTATION OF THESE CONCEPTS FOR YOUR TEAM

Bring me to your company to motivate and inspire your employees to lead a life of tenacious abundance. Remember, I live this every day and have practiced these concepts again and again over the past three decades. In other words, your employees are hearing from the front of the horse, not the other end—LOL!

ABOUT THE AUTHOR

Anthony Trupiano has been happily married, successfully self-employed, and physically healthy for over three decades now. He has found success in the finance and insurance industry for over twenty-one years, though he also worked in health and fitness as well as food and catering. Anthony, thanks to his unending desire for growth and knowledge, has completed dozens of life-improvement programs.

He has also been a speaker at events for organizations such as MassMutual, New York Life, Deutsche Bank, Prudential, Million Dollar Round Table, and NFL Financial Workshop for the Jacksonville Jaguars.

AUTHORS EXPERIENCE AND PROGRAMS ATTENDED

- Married in 5/91, happily married for over thirty-one years

- Self-employed thirty of thirty-one years

- Successful in the health and fitness industry

- Successful in the food and catering industry

- Successful in the financial and insurance industry for over twenty-one years

- High school and collegiate wrestler

Attended the following programs over the past three decades:

- **Tony Robbins** Unleash the Power (twice)

- **Tony Robbins** Date with Destiny

- **Tony Robbins** Wealth Mastery

- **Tony Robbins** Life Mastery
- **Tony Robbins** Business Mastery
- **Richard Bandler** "Master Certification for NLP"
- **Dan Sullivan** "Strategic Coach"
- **Joe Polish** "Genius Network"
- **Peter Diamandis** "Abundance 360"
- **Dr. David Martin** "Integral Asset Management"
- **Keith Cunningham** "Plan or Get Slaughtered"
- **Business Enterprise Institute** "Business Planning Bootcamp"

Online courses:

- **Jim Kwik** "5 Days to a Powerful Memory and Super Brain"
- **Robin Sharma** "Hero, Genius, Legend"
- **Ken Honda** "Money EQ"
- **Marisa Peer** "Abundance and Uncompromised Life"
- **Vishen** "3 Most Important Questions"
- **Steven Kotler** "The Habit of Ferocity"
- **Paul McKenna** "Everyday Bliss"
- **Nir Eyal** "Becoming Focused and Indistractable"
- **Ben Greenfield** "The Longevity Blueprint"
- **Dr. Michael Breus** "The Mastery of Sleep"
- **Dennis Waitley** "The Psychology of Winning"
- **Burt Goldman** "Quantum Jumping"

- **Harvard Online Course** for Business Management and Family Business Generations

Speaker for the following companies/agencies:

- Speaker at Million Dollar Round Table 2009 (in front of 1,650 of top 3% of agents worldwide)
- Speaker for Deutsche Bank
- Speaker for MassMutual
- Speaker New York Life
- Speaker for Waddell & Reid
- Speaker for Prudential
- NFL Financial Workshop for the Jacksonville Jaguars
- National Association of Insurance and Financial Advisors (NAIFA)
- Thirty-day coaching program for the Jacksonville Jaguars with Tom Coughlin and his coaching staff
- Speaker for American Dream U at Fort Benning and Shades of Green

Recommended Products & Vendor Discount Codes

- **Ed Lloyd & Associates CPA** tenacious@elcpa.com
- **Redirect Health** www.redirecthealth.com/tenacious
- **Hypervibe** 10% discount code (enter "tenacious")
- **Platinum red lights** 5% discount code (enter "tenacious")
- **TheraSauna** (use code "Tenacious" for a complimentary accessory kit.)

- **Grounding Mat** www.ultimatelongevity.com/tenacious
- **Grander Water Board** www.vivacityimports.com use code TENACIOUS 5% off
- **PEMF** (see below)

PEMF COUPON CODE LIST

PEMF DEVICE	PEMF DEVICE WEBSITE	DISCOUNT COUPON CODE	COUPON AMOUNT
FlexPulse	www.flexpulse.com	22AT-FP	$50
BioBalance	www.biobalancepemf.com	22AT-BB	$75
TeslaFit +2	www.teslafit.com	22AT-TF+2	$200
TeslaFit Duo	www.teslafit.com	22AT-TFDUO	$400
TeslaFit Pro	www.teslafit.com	22AT-TFPRO	$500
Parmeds Multi Flash	www.drpawluk.com	22AT-MFLASH	$75
Parmeds Premium Flash	www.drpawluk.com	22AT-PFLASH	$100
Parmeds Ultra Flash	www.drpawluk.com	22AT-UFLASH	$100
Parmeds 3D Ultra	www.drpawluk.com	22AT-3DULTRA	$300

TENACIOUS ABUNDANCE

Me and my best friend of over thirty years, Tom Vollers, at Front Sight.

Myself, my dad, and my brother in a photo booth during summer vacation at the New Jersey shore.

Jay Abraham, Marketing Legend, at Genius Network Annual Meeting

Keith Cunningham at his event "Plan or Get Slaughtered"

Sprint Triathlon, Ponte Vedra, Florida

Peter Diamandis at "Abundance 360" Technology Think Tank

Rickson Gracie, "9th Degree Red Belt" of Gracie Ju-jitsu,
undefeated 465—0

Sally Trupiano looking incredible at 55!

Me, Sally and Brianna at Office

Me and my twin brother, John, at Brianna's Wedding

Me with Coach John Wooden at his California home

Me with my daughters, Brianna and Jessica

"Might as well Jump!" Skydived after day two of Anthony Robbins
Personal Power

Me with Sally and Anthony Robbins

Jacksonville Mud Run, eighth place out of seventy-eight racers

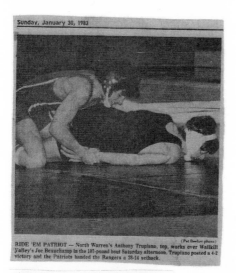

Sunday, January 30, 1983

RIDE 'EM PATRIOT — North Warren's Anthony Trupiano, top, works over Wallkill Valley's Joe Beauchamp in the 107-pound bout Saturday afternoon. Trupiano posted a 4-2 victory and the Patriots handed the Rangers a 28-14 setback. *(Pat Becker photo)*

**North Warren 37,
Sussex Tech 21**

BLAIRSTOWN — Anthony Trupiano's superior decision in the first bout of the afternoon gave North Warren's wrestling team the momentum it needed to hand Sussex Tech a 37-21 setback here Saturday afternoon.

"We were a little surprised with Trupiano's victory at 101," said Patriots coach Bob Seal. "We figured that bout to be a tossup, but Anthony was in control all the way."

Trupiano scored a 12-0 decision over Lou DeLima, setting the stage of North Warren's seventh victory in 12 outings.

Senior Don Quick pushed his record to 14-1 by pinning Tech's Steve Leenheer at 3:03 of the 129 bout. Junior Mike Lehman climbed to 13-1-1 with a forfeit win at 141, and senior Mike Cullen jumped to 16-2 with his fall at 1:28 against Carl Duma in the 188-pound bout.

NORTH WARREN 37
SUSSEX TECH 21
101 Anthony Trupiano (NW) superior decisioned Lou DeLima, 12-0.
108 Bill Gould (ST) decisioned Scott Bedell, 7-1.
115 Dan DeLima (ST) pinned John Trupiano, 1:01.
122 Tom Dugan (NW) won by forfeit.
129 Don Quick (NW) pinned Steve Leenheer, 3:03.
135 Joe DePadua (ST) major decisioned Matt Salmon, 16-1.
141 Mike Lehman (NW) won by forfeit.
148 Greg Salmon (NW) draw with Mark DePadua, 6-6.
158 Gene Makarevich (NW) decisioned Ty Yanvary, 8-3.
170 Frank Schirano (ST) pinned Rich Green, 1:18.
188 Mike Cullen (NW) pinned Carl Duma, 1:28.
HWT Scott Karolchyk (NW) decisioned Jim Meyers, 7-0.
Team records: North Warren (7-5), Sussex Tech (4-9).

**N. Warren 28
Wallkill 14**

HARDYSTON — The Patriots used overall team balance to handle the Rangers Saturday. Wallkill was able to win just four of the 12 individual bouts.

NORTH WARREN 28
WALLKILL VALLEY 14
100 — John Trupiano (N) pinned Scott Hagman, 1:15.
107 — Anthony Trupiano (N) dec. Joe Beauchamp, 4-2.
114 — Pete Vagnik (W) dec. Joe Regasky, 8-2.
121 — Don Quick (N) sup. dec. Pete Golanski, 22-9.
134 — John Regasky (N) draw with Clinton Ish, 2-2.
134 — Ed Greene (W) dec. Matt Salmon, 5-4.
140 — Mike Lehman (N) won by def. over Rod Murray.
147 — Greg Salmon (N) maj. dec. Steve Line, 11-1.
157 — Leo Riccardi (N) dec. Rich Green, 8-6.
167 — Mark VanTassel (W) dec. Gene Makarevich, 7-2.
187 — Mike Cullen (N) pinned Todd Hendricks, 1:38.
HWT — Scott Karolchyk (N) pinned Steve Sofranek, 3:40.
Team Records: North Warren (6-4), Wallkill Valley (2-7-1).

High school wrestling articles. I can't believe I weighed 101 pounds.

Me and Sally on our honeymoon in Cayman Islands with Don Rickles

Wife and Daughter on Brianna's Wedding day

Me with Brianna, Sally before the vows ceremony

Our Yorkie, Sophie, reminds us that GOD spelled backwards is DOG